run-time situation correctly,and in fact most of the graph paths
are not feasible, i.e. do not represent possible executions of the
program. However, this model is widely adopted for two main
reasons: (a) Its relatively simple structure enables us to develop
a comprehensive analytic theory, to construct simple algorithms
which perform the required program analysis and to investigate
general properties of these algorithms in detail (cf. [HE], [AU]
for recent surveys of the subject). (b) Isolation of feasible
paths from non-feasible ones is known to be an undecidable problem,
closely related to the Turing machine halting problem.

This classical technique faces significant problems in the
presence of procedures. These problems reflect the dependence of
individual inter-procedural branches upon each other during program
execution, a dependence which is known at compile time and is
essentially independent of any computation performed during that
execution. Interprocedural branching is thus much easier to
analyze than intra-procedural branches, which usually depend on
the values assumed by various program variables. It is therefore
very tempting to exploit our special knowledge of this branching
pattern in program analysis, thereby tracing the program flow in
a more accurate manner.

Interprocedural flow cannot be treated as a simple extension
of the intra-procedural flow, but calls for a more complicated
model whose mathematical properties require special analysis. In
addition, many programming languages include features such as
procedure variables, and parameter transfer by reference or by
name (cf. [AU]) which complicate the analysis of inter-procedural
flow.

It is therefore not surprising that inter-procedural analysis
has been neglected in much research on data-flow analysis. Most
of the recent literature on this subject virtually ignores any
inter-procedural aspect of the analysis, or splits the inter-
procedural analysis into a preliminary analysis phase which gathers
over-estimated information about the properties of each procedure
in a program and which is followed by an intra-procedural analysis
of each procedure, suppressing any inter-procedural transfer of
control and using instead the previously collected, over-estimated
information to deduce the effects of procedure calls on the program
behavior (cf. [AL2]). These approaches use a relatively simple
model of the program at the expense of some information loss,
arguing that such a loss in intrinsic anyway even in a purely
intra-procedural model.

However, there is a growing feeling among researchers that
more importance should be given to inter-procedural analysis,
especially in deeper analyses with more ambitious goals, where
avoidance of flow over-estimation is likely to be significant in
improving the results of the analysis. This is true in particular
for analyses related to program verification, in which area
several recent papers, notably [DM], [GR], [HA], [GA] and [CO]
have already addressed this issue. We may also mention several
recent works by Rosen [RO], Barth [BA] and Lomet [LO], which
outline some inter-procedural approaches to global data-flow
analysis.

In this paper we introduce two new techniques for performing
inter-procedural analysis of a program as an integral part of its

global flow analysis. These two approaches use two somewhat different graph models for the program being analyzed. The first approach, which we term the <u>functional approach</u> views procedures as collections of structured program blocks, and aims to establish input-output relations for each such block. One then interprets procedure calls as "super operations" whose effect on the program status can be computed using those relations. This approach relates rather closely to most of the known techniques dealing with interprocedural flow, such as the "worst-case assumptions," mixed with processing of procedures in "inverse invocation order" [AL2] Rosen's "indirect arcs" method [RO], in-line expansion of procedures [AL3], as well as most of the known interprocedural techniques for program verification ([GR], [GA], [HA] and [CO]). Our version of this first technique has the advantage of being rather simple to define and implement (admitting very efficient implementations for several important special cases), and is valid even in the presence of recursion. The above mentioned previous approaches to this situation are either much more complicated, or yield only approximate solutions.

Our second technique, which we term the <u>call-strings approach</u> is somewhat orthogonal to the first approach. This second technique blends inter-procedural flow analysis with the analysis of intra-procedural flow, and in effect turns a whole program into a single flow-graph. However, as information is propagated along this graph, it is "tagged" with an encoded history of the procedure calls encountered during propagation. In this way we make inter-procedural flow explicit, and this enables us to determine, when-ever we encounter a procedure return, what part of the information

at hand can validly be propagated through this return, and what part has a conflicting call history, that bars such propagation.

Surprisingly enough, very few techniques using this kind of logic have been suggested up to now. We may note in this connection that a crude approach, but one using similar logic, would be an approach in which procedure calls and returns are interpreted as ordinary branch instructions. Even though the possibility of such an approach has been suggested occasionally in the literature, it has never been considered seriously as an alternative inter-procedural analysis method. A related approach to program verification has been investigated by De-Bakker and Meertens [DM], but, again, this has been quite an isolated attempt, and one having rather discouraging results, which we believe to be due mainly to the ambitious nature of the analyses considered.

We shall show that an appropriate sophistiaction of this approach is in fact quite adequate for data-flow analysis, and gives results quite comparable with those of the functional approach. This latter approach also has the merit that it can easily be transformed into an approximative approach, in which some details of interprocedural flow are lost, but in which the relevant algorithms become much less expensive.

A problem faced by any inter-procedural analysis is the possible presence of recursive procedures. The presence of such procedures causes inter-procedural flow to become much more complex than it is in the non-recursive case, mainly because the length of a sequence of nested calls can be arbitrarily large. Concerning our approaches in this case, we will show that they

always converge in the non-recursive case, but may fail to yield
an effective solution of several data-flow problems (such as constant propagation) for recursive programs. It will also be seen
that much more advanced techniques are needed if we are to cope
fully with recursion for such problems.

We note that it is always possible to transform a program
with procedures into a procedureless program, by converting procedure calls and returns into ordinary branch instructions,
monitored by an explicit stack. If we do this and simply subject
the resulting program to intra-procedural analysis, then we are in
effect ignoring all the delicate properties of the inter-
procedural flow and thus inevitably over-estimating flow. This
simple observation shows that the attempt to perform more accurate
inter-procedural analysis can be viewed as a first (and relatively
easy) step toward accurate analysis of more sophisticated properties of programs than are caught by classical global analysis.

This paper is organized as follows: Section 2 contains preliminary notations and terminology. Section 3 presents the functional approach, first in abstract, definitional terms, and then
shows that it can be effectively implemented for data-flow problems which possess a finite semilattice of possible data values,
and sketch an algorithm for that purpose. We also discuss several
cases in which unusually efficient implementation is possible.
(These cases include many of those considered in classical data-
flow analyses). Section 4 presents the call-strings approach in
abstract, definitional terms showing that it also yields the
solution we desire, though in a manner which is not necessarily
effective in the most general case.   In Section 5 we show that

this latter approach can be effectively implemented if the semilattice of relevant data values is finite, and investigate some of
the efficiency parameters of such an implementation. Section 6
presents a variant of the call strings approach which aims at a
relatively simple, but only approximative, implementation of
interprocedural data-flow analysis.

We would like to express our gratitude to Jacob T. Schwartz
for encouragement and many helpful suggestions and comments concerning this research.

2. Notations and Terminology

In this section we will review various basic notations and terminology used in intra-procedural analysis, which will be referred to, and modified, subsequently. The literature on data-flow analysis is by now quite extensive, and we refer the reader to [HE[or [AU], two excellent recent introductory expositions of that subject.

To analyse a program consisting of several subprocedures, each subprocedure p, including the main program, is first divided into basic blocks. An (extended) basic block is a maximal single-entry multi-exit sequence of code. For convenience, we will assume that each procedure call constitutes a single-instruction block. We also assume that each subprocedure p has a unique exit block, denoted by e_p, which is also assumed to be a single-instruction block, and also that p has a unique entry (root) block, denoted by r_p.

Assume for the moment that p contains no procedure calls. Then the flow-graph G_p of p is a rooted directed graph whose nodes are the basic blocks of p, whose root is r_p, and which contains an edge (m,n) iff there is a direct transfer of control from the basic block m to (the start of) the basic block n, effected by some branch instruction. The presence of calls in p induces several possible inter-procedural extensions of the flow-graph, which will be discussed in the next section.

Let G be any rooted directed graph. G is denoted by a triplet (N,E,r) where N is the set of its nodes, E the set of edges and r its root. A <u>path</u> p in G is a sequence of nodes in N $(n_1, n_2, \ldots, n_k)$ such that for each $1 \leq j < k$, $(n_j, n_{j+1}) \in E$. p is said to lead from n_1 (its initial node) to n_k (its terminal node). p can be also represented as the corresponding sequence of edges $((n_1, n_2), \ldots, (n_{k-1}, n_k))$. The <u>length</u> of p is defined as the number of edges along p (k-1 in the above notation). For each pair of nodes m, n $\in$ N we define $path_G(m,n)$ as the set of all paths in G, leading from m to n.

We assume that the program to be analyzed is written in a programming language with the following semantic properties: Procedure parameters are transferred by value, rather than by reference or by name (so that we can, and will, ignore the problem of "aliasing" discussed by Rosen [RO]) and there are no procedure variables or external procedures. We also assume that the program has been translated into an intermediate-level code in which the transfer of values between actual arguments and formal parameters of a procedure is explicit in the code and is accomplished by argument-transmitting assignments, inserted before and after procedure calls. Because of this last assumption, formal parameters can be treated in the same way as other global variables. All these assumptions are made in order to simplify our treatment and are rather reasonable. If the first two assumptions are not satisfied then things get much more complicated, though not beyond control. The third assumption is rather arbitrary but most convenient. (In [CO], e.g., the converse assumption is made, namely

that global variables are passed between procedures as parameters,
an assumption which we believe to be less favorable technically.)

A global data-flow framework is defined to be a pair (L,F),
where L is a semilattice of data- or attribute-information and F
is a space of functions acting in L (and describing a possible
way in which data may propagate along program flow). Let $\wedge$ denote
the semilattice operation of L (called a meet), which is assumed
to be idempotent, associative and commutative. We assume that L
contains a smallest element, denoted by 0 (usually signifying
null information (see below). F is assumed to be closed under
functional composition and meet, to contain an identity map, and
to be monotone, i.e. to be such that for each $f \in F$, x, $y \in L$,
$x \leq y$ implies $f(x) \leq f(y)$. L is also assumed to be bounded, i.e.
not to contain any infinite decreasing sequence of distinct elements. (L,F) is called a distributive framework if, for each
$f \in F$ and x, $y \in L$, $f(x \wedge y) = f(x) \wedge f(y)$.

Given a global data-flow framework (L,F) and a flow graph G,
we associate with each edge (m,n) of G a propagation function
$f_{(m,n)} \in F$, which represents the change of relevant data-attributes
as control passes from the start of m, through m, to the start of
n. (Recall that a basic block may have more than one exit, so that
$f_{(m,n)}$ must depend on n as well as m.

Once the set $S = \{f_{(m,n)}: (m,n) \in E\}$ is given, we can define
a (graph-dependent) space F of propagation functions as the
smallest set of functions acting in L which contains S and the
identity map, and which is closed under functional compositions
and meets. It is clear that this F is monotone iff S is monotone,

and that F is distributive iff S is distributive.

Once F is defined, we can formulate the following general set of data-propagation equations, where, for each $n \in N$, x_n denotes the data available at the start of n:

$$x_r = 0$$

(2.1)

$$x_n = \bigwedge_{(m,n) \in E} f_{(m,n)} (x_m) , \quad n \in N - \{r\}$$

These equations describe attribute propagation "locally," i.e. they show the relation between attributes collected at adjacent basic blocks, starting with null information at the program entry.

The solutions of these equations approximate the following abstractly defined function known as the <u>meet over all paths</u> solution to an optimisation problem

(2.2) $\qquad y_n = \bigwedge \{f_p(0) : p \in \text{path}_G(r,n)\} , \quad n \in N ;$

here we define $f_p = f_{(n_{k-1}, n_k)} \circ f_{(n_{k-2}, n_{k-1})} \cdots \circ f_{(n_1, n_2)}$ for each path $p = (n_1, n_2, \ldots, n_k)$. If p is null, then f_p is defined to be the identity map on L.

Many algorithms which solve equations (2.1) are known by now. These algorithms fall into two main categories: (i) iterative algorithms, which use only functional applications (cf. [KI], [HU], [KU2], [HE], [TA1]). (ii) elimination algorithms, which also use functional compositions and meets (cf. [CA], [GW], [TA2]). All these algorithms yield the maximal fixed point solution to equations (2.1), which does coincide with the solution (2.2)

provided that the data-flow framework in question is distributive [KI], but which may fail to do so if the framework is only monotone [KU1]. However, in which case, even in this latter case we still have $x_n \leq y_n$ for all $n \in N$, i.e. obtain an under-estimated solution, which is always a safe one (cf. [HE]). In what follows, we will assume some basic knowledge of these classical optimisation algorithms.

3. The functional approach to interprocedural analysis

In this section we present our first approach to interprocedural analysis. This approach treats each procedure as a structure of blocks, which establishes relations between attribute data
at its entry and related data at any of its nodes. Using these
relations, attribute data is propagated directly through each
procedure call.

We prepare for our description by giving some definitions and
making some observations concerning the inter-procedural nature
of general programs. Let us first introduce the notion of an
interprocedural flow graph of a computer program containing several procedures. We can consider two alternative representations
of such a graph G. In the first representation, we have $G = \cup \{G_p : p$ is a procedure in the program$\}$, where, for each p,
$G_p = (N_p, E_p, r_p)$, and where r_p is the entry block of p, N_p is the
set of all basic blocks within p, and $E_p = E_p^0 \cup E_p^1$ is the set of
edges of G_p. An edge $(m,n) \in E_p^0$ iff there can be a direct transfer of control from m to n (via a 'go-to' or 'if' statement,
and $(m,n) \in E_p^1$ iff m is a call block and n is the block immediately
following that call.

Thus this representation, which is the one to be used ex-
plicitly in our first approach, separates the flow graphs of
individual procedures from each other.

A second representation, denoted by G^*, is defined as follows:
$G^* = (N^*, E^*, r_1)$, where $N^* = \cup N_p$, and $E^* = E^0 \cup E^1$, where $E^0 = \cup_p E_p^0$ and an edge $(m,n) \in E^1$ iff either m is a call block and n is

the entry block of the called procedure (in which case (m,n) is called a <u>call edge</u>), or if m is an exit block of some procedure p and n is a block immediately following a call to p (in which case (m,n) is called a <u>return edge</u>). The call edge (m,r_p) and a return edge (e_q,n) are said to <u>correspond</u> to each other if p=q and (m,n) ϵ E_s^1, for some procedure s. Here r_1 is the entry block of the main program, sometimes also denoted as r_{main}. Of course, not all paths through G* are (even statically) feasible, in the sense of representing potentially valid execution paths, since the definition of G* ignores the special nature of procedure calls and returns. For each n ϵ N* we define $IVP(r_1,n)$ as the set of all inter-procedurally valid paths in G* which lead from r_1 to n. A path q ϵ $path_{G*}(r_1,n)$ is in $IVP(r_1,n)$ iff the sequence of all edges in q which are in E^1, which we will write as q_1 or $q|_{E_1}$, is <u>proper</u> in the following recursive sense:

(i) A tuple q_1 which contains no return edges is proper.

(ii) If q_1 contains return edges, and i is the smallest index in q_1 such that $q_1(i)$ is a return edge, then q_1 is proper if i>1 and $q_1(i-1)$ is a call edge corresponding to the return edge $q_1(i)$, and after deleting those two components from q_1, the remaining tuple is also proper.

<u>Remark</u>: It is interesting to note that the set of all proper tuples over E^1, as well as $\underset{n}{\cup}\ IVP(r_1,n)$, can be generated by a context-free grammar (but not by a regular grammar), in contrast with the set of all possible paths in G*, which is regular.

For each procedure p and each n ϵ N_p, we also define $IVP_0(r_p,n)$ as the set of all interprocedurally valid paths q in

G^* from r_p to n such that each procedure call in q is completed
by a subsequent corresponding return edge in q. More precisely,
a path $q \in path_{G^*}(r_p,n)$ is in $IVP_o(r_p,n)$ iff $q_1 = q|_{E^1}$ is <u>complete</u>,
in the following recursive sense.

(i) The null tuple is complete.

(ii) A tuple q_1 is complete if it is either a concatenation of two
     complete subtuples, or else it starts with a call edge,
     terminates with the corresponding return edge, and the rest
     of its components constitute a complete subtuple.

The notions introduced above appear in the following Path
Decomposition Lemma:

<u>Lemma 3.1</u>: Let $n \in N^*$ and $q \in IVP(r_1,n)$. Then there exist pro-
cedures $p_1,p_2,\ldots,p_j$, where p_1 is the main program and p_j the procedure containing n, and calls $c_1,\ldots,c_{j-1}$ such that for each $i<j$
c_i is in p_i and calls p_{i+1}, and q can be represented as

(3.1) $q = q_1||(c_1,r_{p_2})||q_2||\ldots||(c_{j-1},r_{p_j})||q_j$

where for each $i<j$ $q_i \in IVP_o(r_{p_i},c_i)$ and $q_j \in IVP_o(r_{p_j},n)$.
Conversely, any path which admits such a decomposition is in
$IVP(r_1,n)$. Moreover, this decomposition is unique.

<u>Proof</u>: Let $q^* = q|_{E^1}$. If q^* is empty, then q^* is also complete,
so that $q \in IVP_o(r_1,n)$, and we have the trivial decomposition
q=q with j=1 (n must belong to the main program in this case).

Otherwise, in view of the definition of a proper E^1-tuple,
and by making repeated deletions of adjacent call edges and
corresponding return edges, we can reduce q^* to a tuple q^{**} which

is either a null tuple or a non-empty tuple containing only call edges. Let j = length of q^{**} + 1. If $j=1$, i.e. if q^{**} is empty, it is readily seen that q^* is complete and that n belongs to the main program, and we have again the trivial decomposition $q=q$.

If $j > 1$, let $c_i = q^{**}(i)(1)$, $i=1,\ldots,j-1$, and put p_1 = main program, p_{i+1} = the procedure called from c_i, $i=1,\ldots,j-1$. In view of the way in which q^{**} was obtained from q, it follows that c_i is in p_i for each $i < j$. Let $m_o=1$ and m_i be the original index of $q^{**}(i)$ in q, $i=1,\ldots,j-1$. Then we have the decomposition $q = q_1 || (c_1, r_{p_2}) || q_2 \cdots || (c_{j-1}, r_{p_j}) || q_j$ where $q_i = q(m_{i-1}+1 : m_i - 1)$, $i=1,\ldots,j-1$, and $q_j = q(m_{j-1}+1:)$. [*] It is easily verified that $q_i \big|_{E^1}$ is complete for each $i \leq j$, and therefore $q_i \in IVP_o(r_{p_i}, c_i)$ for $i < j$ and $q_j \in IVP_o(r_{p_j}, n)$.

The proof of the converse assertion is simpler, and follows directly from the definitions of IVP and IVP_o.

The uniqueness of this decomposition is also easy to establish, since $c_1,\ldots,c_{j-1}$ are precisely all the calls along q which are not subsequently completed, and it is fairly obvious from the definitions that these calls and their positions in q are unique, which immediately implies the uniqueness of the whole decomposition.

$$\text{Q.E.D.}$$

We can now describe our 'functional' approach to interprocedural analysis. Let (L,F) be a distributive data-flow framework for G. In the first phase of the functional approach we take F

[*] _footnote_: for any tuple or string a, $a(i:j)$ denotes its subpart from the i-th component to the j-th one, inclusive; $a(i:)$ denotes the subpart of a from the i-th component to its end.

as the direct basis for our analysis. More precisely, for each procedure p and each $n \in N_p$, we define an element $\phi_{(r_p,n)} \in F$ which describes the manner in which attributes in L are propagated from the start of r_p to the start of n along paths in $IVP_o(r_p,n)$. These functions must satisfy the following (non-linear) set of equations, whose heuristic meaning should be self-explanatory: For each $(m,n) \in E^o$, let $f_{(m,n)} \in F$ denote the associated propagation effect. Then

$$\phi_{(r_p,r_p)} = id_L, \quad \text{for each procedure p}$$

(3.2)

$$\phi_{(r_p,n)} = \bigwedge_{(m,n) \in E_p} (h_{(m,n)} \circ \phi_{(r_p,m)}), \quad \text{for each } n \in N_p - \{r_p\}$$

where

$$h_{(m,n)} = \begin{cases} f_{(m,n)} & \text{if } (m,n) \in E_p^o \\ \\ \phi_{(r_q,e_q)} & \text{if } (m,n) \in E_p^1 \text{ and m calls procedure q} \end{cases}$$

This set of equations possesses a maximal fixed point solution which is defined as follows: Let F be ordered by writing $g_1 \geq g_2$ for g_1, $g_2 \in F$ iff $g_1(x) \geq g_2(x)$ for all $x \in L$. (We will assume that L contains a maximal element Ω which denotes a totally undefined attribute, and that F contains a function f_Ω which maps each $x \in L$ into Ω, so that f_Ω is the largest element in F.)

Start by putting

$$\phi^o_{(r_p,r_p)} = id_L, \quad \text{for each procedure p}$$

$$\phi^o_{(r_p,n)} = f_\Omega, \quad \text{for each } n \in N_p - \{r_p\}$$

and then apply Equations (3.2) iteratively in a round robin fashion
to obtain new approximations to the ϕ's. (This can be done using
iterations either of Gauss-Seidel type of Jacobi's type, though the
former is a better approach.) Let $\phi^i_{(r_p,n)}$ denote the i-th approximation computed in this manner. Since $\phi^0_{(r_p,n)} \geq \phi^1_{(r_p,n)}$ for all
p, n, it follows inductively that $\phi^i_{(r_p,n)} \geq \phi^{i+1}_{(r_p,n)}$ for each p, n
and $i \geq 0$.

A problem which arises here is that F need not in general be
a bounded semilattice, even if L is bounded. If L is finite then
F must be finite and therefore bounded, but if L is not finite, F
need not in general be bounded.

Nevertheless, even if the sequence $\{\phi^j_{(r_p,n)}\}_{j \geq 0}$ is infinite for
some p, n we still can define its limit, denoted by $\varphi_{(r_p,n)}$, as
follows: For each $x \in L$, the sequence $\{\phi^j_{(r_p,n)}(x)\}_{j \geq 0}$ is decreasing in L, and since L is bounded, it must be finite, and we define
$\varphi_{(r_p,n)}(x)$ as its limit. (To ensure that $\varphi_{(r_p,n)} \in F$ we must
impose another condition upon F, namely: for each decreasing
sequence $\{g_i\}_{i \geq 0}$ of functions in F, the limit defined as above is
also in F.) Thus, the above process defined a solution
$\{\varphi_{(r_p,n)}\}_{p,n}$ to equations (3.2) though not necessarily effectively.
It is easy to check that the limiting functions defined by the
iterative process that we have described are indeed a solution,
and that in fact it is the maximal fixed point solution of (3.2).

Having obtained this solution, we can use it to compute a
solution to our data-flow problem. For each basic block n let
$x_n \in L$ denote the information available at the start of n. Then
we have the following set of equations:

(a) $x_{r_{main}} = 0 \in L$

(3.3) (b) for each procedure p,

$$x_{r_p} = \bigwedge \{\phi_{(r_q, c)}(x_{r_q}) : q \text{ is a procedure and} \\ c \text{ is a call to p in q}\}$$

(c) $x_n = \phi_{(r_p, n)}(x_{r_p})$, for each procedure p, and $n \in N_p - \{r_p\}$

These equations can be (effectively) solved by a standard iterative algorithm, which yields the maximal fixed point solution of (3.3).

We illustrate the above procedure for solution of equations (3.2) and (3.3) by the following example, in which we suppose that available expressions analysis is to be performed:

Example 1

```
main program          procedure p
read a, b;            if a = 0 then return;
t := a*b;             else
call p;                 a := a - 1;
t := a*b;               call p;
print t;                t := a*b;
stop;                 end if;
end;                  return;
                      end;
```

Our interprocedural analysis will show that a*b is available upon exit from the recursive procedure p, so that its second computation in the main program is redundant and can therefore be eliminated. (Traditional inter-procedural methods will usually fail to detect this fact, since the expression a*b is killed in p.)

We now exhibit the details of the iterative solution of equations (3.2) and (3.3) for this above program P. Our first solution step transforms P into the following interprocedural flow graph (where solid arrows denote intra-procedural edges, dotted arrows denote edges in $\cup \ E^1_p$, and dashed arrows denote interprocedural edges, i.e. edges in E^1):

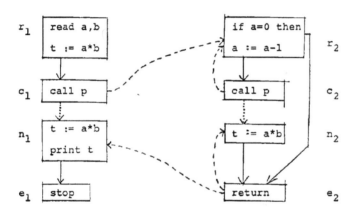

For simplicity we will only show that part of the analysis, which pertains directly to the single expression a*b. Assuming this simplification, $L = \{0,1,\Omega\}$, where 1 indicates that a*b is available and 0 that it is not, and each $f \in F$ can be denoted by a pair (a,b), where $a = f(0)$, $b = f(1)$ (recall that $f(\Omega) = \Omega$ always), so that e.g. $id_L = (0,1)$. With these notations, equations (3.2) read

$$\phi_{(r_1,r_1)} = (0,1)$$
$$\phi_{(r_2,r_2)} = (0,1)$$
$$\phi_{(r_1,c_1)} = (1,1) \circ \phi_{(r_1,r_1)}$$

$$\phi_{(r_1,n_1)} = \phi_{(r_2,e_2)} \circ \phi_{(r_1,c_1)}$$

$$\phi_{(r_1,e_1)} = (1,1) \circ \phi_{(r_1,n_1)}$$

$$\phi_{(r_2,c_2)} = (0,0) \circ \phi_{(r_2,r_2)}$$

$$\phi_{(r_2,n_2)} = \phi_{(r_2,e_2)} \circ \phi_{(r_2,c_2)}$$

$$\phi_{(r_2,e_2)} = [(0,1) \circ \phi_{(r_2,r_2)}] \bigwedge [(1,1) \circ \phi_{(r_2,n_2)}]$$

The following table summarizes the iterative solution of these equations:

function	initial value	after 1 iteration	2 iterations	3 iterations
$\phi_{(r_1,r_1)}$	$(0,1)$	$(0,1)$	$(0,1)$	$(0,1)$
$\phi_{(r_1,c_1)}$	(Ω,Ω)	$(1,1)$	$(1,1)$	$(1,1)$
$\phi_{(r_1,n_1)}$	(Ω,Ω)	(Ω,Ω)	$(1,1)$	$(1,1)$
$\phi_{(r_1,e_1)}$	(Ω,Ω)	(Ω,Ω)	$(1,1)$	$(1,1)$
$\phi_{(r_2,r_2)}$	$(0,1)$	$(0,1)$	$(0,1)$	$(0,1)$
$\phi_{(r_2,c_2)}$	(Ω,Ω)	$(0,0)$	$(0,0)$	$(0,0)$
$\phi_{(r_2,n_2)}$	(Ω,Ω)	(Ω,Ω)	$(0,0)$	$(0,0)$
$\phi_{(r_2,e_2)}$	(Ω,Ω)	$(0,1)$	$(0,1)$	$(0,1)$

Thus, the first stage of one solution stabilizes after 3 iterations. Next we solve equations (3.3), which read as follows:

(a)
$$x_{r_1} = 0$$

(b)
$$x_{r_2} = \phi_{(r_1,c_1)}(x_{r_1}) \bigwedge \phi_{(r_2,c_2)}(x_{r_2})$$

$$= (1,1)(x_{r_1}) \bigwedge (0,0)(x_{r_2})$$

For these equations we see after two iterations that

$$x_{r_1} = x_{r_2} = 0$$

from which, using (3.3) (c), we obtain the complete solution

$$x_{r_1} = x_{r_2} = x_{c_2} = x_{n_2} = x_{e_2} = 0$$

$$x_{c_1} = x_{n_1} = x_{e_1} = 1$$

i.e. a*b is available at the start of n_1, which is what we wanted
to show.

Next we shall analyze the properties of the solution of
equations (3.2) and (3.3) as defined above. As in intra-procedural
analysis our main objective is to show that this solution coincides
with the meet over all paths solution defined (in the interprocedural case) as follows:

(3.4) $\psi_n = \bigwedge \{f_q : q \in IVP(r_{main}, n)\} \in F$, for each $n \in N^*$

(3.5) $y_n = \psi_n(0)$, for each $n \in N^*$ (this is the meet over all paths
solution).

<u>Lemma 3.2</u>: Let $n \in N_p$ for some procedure p. Then

$$\phi_{(r_p, n)} = \bigwedge \{f_q : q \in IVP_o(r_p, n)\}$$

<u>Proof</u>: We first prove, by induction on i, that for all $i \geq 0$

$$\phi^i_{(r_p, n)} \geq \bigwedge \{f_q : q \in IVP_o(r_p, n)\}$$

Indeed, for i=0, if $n = r_p$ then $\phi^o_{(r_p, r_p)} = id_L = f_{q_o}$, where
$q_o \in IVP_o(r_p, r_p)$ is the empty path from r_p to r_p, so that
$\phi^o_{(r_p, r_p)} \geq \bigwedge \{f_q : q \in IVP_o(r_p, r_p)\}$. If $n \neq r_p$ then $\phi^o_{(r_p, n)} = f_\Omega \geq f$

for all $f \in F$. Thus the assertion is true for $i=0$.

Suppose that it is true for some i. For either kind of iterative computation of the functions ϕ^{i+1} using equations (3.2) we have

$$\phi^{i+1}_{(r_p,n)} \geq \bigwedge_{(m,n) \in E_p} (h_{(m,n)} \circ \phi^i_{(r_p,m)})$$

$$\geq \bigwedge_{(m,n) \in E_p} (h_{(m,n)} \circ \bigwedge \{f_q : q \in IVP_0(r_p,m)\})$$

for each procedure p and $n \in N_p - \{r_p\}$. (Note here that if $n = r_p$, then $\phi^{i+1}_{(r_p,n)} = \phi^1_{(r_p,n)} = \phi^0_{(r_p,n)} \geq \{f_q : q \in IVP_0(r_p,n)\}$. Our chain of equalities and inequalities then continues:)

$$= \bigwedge_{(m,n) \in E^0_p} (f_{(m,n)} \circ \bigwedge \{f_q : q \in IVP_0(r_p,m)\}) \bigwedge$$

$$\bigwedge_{\substack{(m,n) \in E^1_p \\ m \text{ calls } p'}} (\phi^i_{(r_{p'},e_{p'})} \circ \bigwedge \{f_q : q \in IVP_0(r_p,m)\})$$

$$\geq \bigwedge_{(m,n) \in E^0_p} (\bigwedge \{f_q \| (m,n) : q \in IVP_0(r_p,m)\}) \bigwedge$$

$$\bigwedge_{\substack{(m,n) \in E^1_p \\ m \text{ is a call} \\ \text{to } p'}} (\bigwedge \{f_{q'} : q' \in IVP_0(r_{p'},e_{p'})\}) \circ \bigwedge \{f_q : q \in IVP_0(r_p,m)\})$$

$$= \bigwedge_{(m,n) \in E^0_p} (\bigwedge \{f_q \| (m,n) : q \in IVP_0(r_p,m)\}) \bigwedge$$

$$\bigwedge_{\substack{(m,n) \in E^1_p \\ m \text{ is a call} \\ \text{to } p'}} (\bigwedge \{f_q \| (m,r_{p'}) \| q' \| (e_{p'},n) : q \in IVP_0(r_p,m), \\ q' \in IVP_0(r_{p'},e_{p'})\})$$

It is easily checked that for each function f_{q_1} appearing in the

last right-hand side, $q_1 \in IVP_o(r_p,n)$. Hence, this last right-hand side must be

$$\geq \{f_q : q \in IVP_o(r_p,n)\}$$

The same inequality is then seen to apply to the limit function $\phi_{(r_p,n)}$ as well.

To prove inequality in the other direction, we will show that for each $q \in IVP_o(r_p,n)$, $f_q \geq \phi_{(r_p,n)}$. This will be proven by induction on the length of q. If this length is 0 then n must be equal to r_p and $f_q = \phi_{(r_p,r_p)} = id_L$. Suppose that the assertion is true for all p, n and all $q \in IVP_o(r_p,n)$ whose length $\leq k$, and let there be given p, n, q such that the length of q is k+1. Let (m,n) be the last edge in q, so that we can write $q = q_1 || (m,n)$.

If $(m,n) \in E_p^o$ then $q_1 \in IVP_o(r_p,m)$ and its length is $\leq k$. Therefore $f_{q_1} \geq \phi_{(r_p,m)}$ and by (3.2) we have

$$f_q = f_{(m,n)} \circ f_{q_1} \geq h_{(m,n)} \circ \phi_{(r_p,m)} \geq \phi_{(r_p,n)}$$

If $(m,n) \in E^1$, then $m = e_{p'}$ for some procedure p'. It is easily seen from the definition of IVP_o, that q can be decomposed as $q_1 || (m_1,r_{p'}) || q_2 || (e_{p'},n)$, such that $(m_1,n) \in E_p^1$, $q_1 \in IVP_o(r_p,m_1)$, $q_2 \in IVP_o(r_{p'},e_{p'})$. Since $f_{(m_1,r_{p'})} = f(e_{p'},n) = id_L$ (since m_1 and $e_{p'}$ are single instruction blocks, containing only an interprocedural branch instruction), we have

$$f_q = f_{q_2} \circ f_{q_1}$$

But both q_1 and q_2 have length $\leq k$, so that by (3.2) and the induction hypothesis, we obtain

$$f_q \geq \phi_{(r_{p'},e_{p'})} \circ \phi_{(r_p,m_1)} = h_{(m_1,n)} \circ \phi_{(r_p,m_1)} \geq \phi_{(r_p,n)}$$

This proves our assertion, from which the lemma follows immediately.

Q.E.D.

Let us now define, for each basic block n,

(3.6) $\quad \chi_n = \bigwedge \{ \phi_{(r_{p_j},n)} \circ \phi_{(r_{p_{j-1}},c_{j-1})} \circ \cdots \circ \phi_{(r_{p_1},c_1)} :$

$\quad\quad\quad p_1$ = main program, p_j is the procedure containing n,

$\quad\quad\quad$ and for each $1 < j$ c_i is a call to p_{i+1} from $p_i \}$

(3.7) $\quad\quad\quad\quad\quad\quad z_n = \bar{\chi}_n(0)$

<u>Theorem 3.3</u>: $\psi_n = \chi_n$ for each $n \in N^*$.

<u>Proof</u>: Let $q \in IVP(r_{main},n)$. By Lemma 3.1 q admits a decomposi-
tion $q = q_1 || (c_1,r_{p_2}) || q_2 || \ldots || (c_{j-1},r_{p_j}) || q_j$ as in (3.1), i.e.
there exist procedures p_1 = main program, $p_2, \ldots, p_j$ = the procedure containing n, and calls $c_1, \ldots, c_{j-1}$ such that for each $1 < j$
c_i is a call to p_{i+1} from p_i, and $q_i \in IVP_0(r_{p_i},c_i)$, and also
$q_j \in IVP_0(r_{p_j},n)$.

Thus, by Lemma 3.2, we have

$$f_q = f_{q_j} \circ f_{q_{j-1}} \circ \cdots \circ f_{q_1} \geq \phi_{(r_{p_j},n)} \circ \phi_{(r_{p_{j-1}},c_{j-1})} \circ \cdots \circ \phi_{(r_{p_1},c_1)}$$

$$\geq \chi_n$$

Hence, $\psi_n \geq \chi_n$.

Conversely, let $p_1, \ldots, p_j, c_1, \ldots, c_{j-1}$ be as in (3.6). By
lemma 3.2 we have

$$\phi(r_{p_j},n)^{\circ} \ \phi(r_{p_{j-1}},c_{j-1})^{\circ} \ \cdots \ \circ \phi(r_{p_1},c_1) \ =$$

$$\bigwedge \{f_{q_j} \circ f_{q_{j-1}} \circ \cdots \circ f_{q_1} : q_i \in IVP_0(r_{p_1},c_i) \text{ for each } i<j \text{ and}$$

$$q_j \in IVP_0(r_{p_j},n)\}$$

$$= \ \{f_{q_1||(c_1,r_{p_2})||q_2\ldots||(c_{j-1},r_{p_j})||q_j} : \text{ same as above}\}$$

By Lemma 3.1, each concatenated path in the last set expression belongs to $IVP(r_{main},n)$. Thus, the last expression is

$$\geq \bigwedge \{f_q : q \in IVP(r_{main},n)\} = \psi_n$$

Therefore $\chi_n \geq \psi_n$ so that χ_n and ψ_n are equal for each $n \in N^*$.

Q.E.D.

We can now prove our main result:

<u>Theorem 3.4</u>: For each basic block $n \in N^*$, $x_n = y_n = z_n$.

<u>Proof</u>: It is immediate from Theorem 3.3 that $y_n = z_n$ for each $n \in N^*$. We claim that $x_{r_p} = z_{r_p}$ for all procedures p in the program. By (3.3)(c), (3.6) and (3.7) this will imply that $x_n = z_n$ for all n.

To prove our claim, we define a new flow graph $G_c = (N_c, E_c, r_1)$, where: N_c is the set of all entry blocks and call blocks in the program.

$E_c = E_c^0 + E_c^1$ is the set of edges of G_c. An edge $(m,n) \in E_c^0$ iff m is the entry of some procedure p and n is a call within p. Moreover, $(m,n) \in E_c^1$ iff m is a call to some procedure p and n is the entry of p. As before, r_1 is the entry block of the main program. We now define a data-flow problem for G_c by associating a data-propagating map $g_{(m,n)} \in F$ with each $(m,n) \in E_c$, in

such a way that

$$g_{(m,n)} = \begin{cases} \phi_{(m,n)} & \text{if } (m,n) \in E_c^o \\ \text{id}_L & \text{if } (m,n) \in E_c^1 \end{cases}$$

It is clear that equations (3.3)(a), (3.3)(b) are equivalent to
the iterative equations for the new data-flow problem. On the
other hand, equations (3.6) and (3.7) define the meet over all
paths solution for the same problem, if we substitute only entry
blocks or call blocks for n. Since F is assumed to be distributive, it follows by Kildall's theorem [KI], that $x_{r_p} = z_{r_p}$ for
each procedure p, and this completes the proof of our theorem.

$$\hspace{8cm} \text{Q.E.D.}$$

It is now time to discuss the pragmatic problems that will
affect attempts to use the functional approach to interprocedural
analysis that we have sketched. The main problem is, obviously,
how to compute the ϕ's effectively if L is not finite (or if F is
not bounded). As examples below will show, in the most general
case the functional approach does not and cannot yield an effective
algorithm for solving equations (3.2) and (3.3). Moreover, even
if the iterative computation of the ϕ's converges, we must still
face the problem of space needed to represent these functions.
Since the functional method that we have outlined manipulates the
ϕ's directly, instead of just applying them to elements of L, it
can increase the space required for data-flow analysis if L is
finite, and may even fail to give finite representation to the ϕ's,
if L is infinite. We note here that our functional approach
belongs to the class of elimination algorithms for solving data-
flow problems (a class of methods which includes the interval-

oriented algorithms of Cocke and Allen [CA], and Tarjan's fast
elimination algorithms [TA2]), since it uses functional compositions
and meets in addition to functional applications. All such elimination algorithms face similar problems, and in practical terms are
therefore limited to cases in which the elements of F possess some
compact and simple representation, and in which F is a bounded semilattice. This family of cases includes the classical data-flow problems (i.e. analysis for available expressions, use-definition
chaining, etc.; cf. [HE]).

It is interesting to ask whether it is possible to modify the
functional approach so that it avoids explicit functional compositions and meets, and thus becomes an iterative approach. This is
possible if L is finite, and an implementation having this property
will be sketched below.

The following example will illustrate some of the pragmatic
problems noted above, and also some potential advantages of the
functional approach over any iterative variant of it. Suppose that
we want to perform constant propagation (see e.g. [HE] for a description of the standard framework used in this analysis). Consider
the following code:

Example 2

```
main program          procedure p
A := 0;               if cond then
call P;                   A := A+1;
print A;                  call p;
end;                      A := A-1;

                      end if;
                      return; end;
```

If we do not allow symbolic representation of the ϕ's, then, in any iterative approach, we shall have to compute $\phi_{(r_p,e_p)}(\{(A,0)\})$, for which we need to compute (for the second level of recursion) $\phi_{(r_p,e_p)}(\{(A,1)\})$ etc., computing $\phi_{(r_p,e_p)}(\{(A,k)\})$ for all integers $k \geq 0$. Thus, an iterative approach would diverge in this example.

However, if symbolic or some other compact representation of the ϕ's is possible, then it can be advantageous to manipulate these functions directly, without applying them to elements of L till their final value has been obtained. This can give us an overall description of their behaviour, allowing them to be calculated in relatively few iterations. For example, in the example shown above, it is easily checked that $\phi_{(r_p,e_p)}$ is found to be id_L after two iterations.

However, convergence of the purely functional approach is not ensured in general. To see this, consider the following slight modification of the preceding example.

Example 3

```
main program          procedure p

A := 0;               if cond then

call p;                  A := A+2+sign(A-100),

print A;                 call p;

end;                     A := A-1;

                      end if;

                      return; end;
```

It is fairly easy to check that the purely functional approach (which uses symbolic representation of the ϕ's) will diverge if negative integers are included in the program domain. Intuitively,

this is due to the fact that it takes more than 100+k iterations through Equations (3.2) to detect that $\phi_{(r_p, e_p)}(\{(A, -k)\}) = \emptyset$ for all $k \geq 0$.

Remark: The data-flow framework required for constant propagation is in general not distributive. However, it can be shown that the standard framework for constant propagation becomes distributive if the program contains only one single variable and each propagation between adjacent basic blocks either sets the value of that variable to some constant, or calculates the output value of the variable from its input value in a one-one manner, as in the above examples.

These examples indicate that if L is not finite, divergence can actually occur. If L is infinite but F is bounded, then a symbolic functional approach would converge, whereas an iterative approach could still diverge if infinite space were needed to represent the ϕ's. Moreover, we have at present no simple criterion which guarantees that F is bounded in cases in which L is infinite. For these reasons, we will henceforth assume that L is a finite semilattice. We can then summarize our results up to this point as follows:

Corollary 3.5: If (L,F) is a distributive data-flow framework and the semilattice L is finite, then the iterative solution of Equations (3.2) converges, and together with Equations (3.3) yields the meet over all interprocedurally valid paths solution (3.5).

Next we shall sketch an algorithm which implements the functional approach for frameworks with a finite semilattice L. We do not assume that any compact representation for elements of F is

available, but instead give purely iterative representation to the
functional approach, which avoids all functional compositions and meets
and also computes the ϕ's only for values which reach some relevant
procedure entry during propagation.

Our algorithm is workpile-driven. The functions ϕ are represented by a two-dimensional partially defined map PHI: $N^* \times L \to L$,
so that for each $n \in N^*$, $x \in L$, PHI(n,x) represents $\phi_{(r_p,n)}(x)$, where
p is the procedure containing n. The substeps of the algorithm are
as follows:

1. Initialize WORK := $\{(r_1,0)\}$, PHI$(r_1,0)$:= 0. (WORK is a subset
of $N^* \times L$, containing pairs (n,x) for which PHI(n,x) has been changed
and its new value has not yet been propagated to successor blocks of
n.)

2. While WORK $\neq \emptyset$, remove an element (n,x) from WORK, and let
    y = PHI(n,x).

    (a) If n is a call block in a procedure q, calling a procedure
    p, then

        (i) If z = PHI(e_p,y) is defined, let m be the unique block
        such that $(n,m) \in E_q^1$, and propagate (x,z) to m. (By this
        we mean: assign PHI(m,x) := PHI$(m,x) \wedge z$, where undefined
        PHI(m,x) is interpreted as Ω; if the value of PHI(m,x) has
        changed, add (m,x) to WORK.)

        (ii) Otherwise, propagate (y,y) to r_p. This will trigger
        propagation through p, which will later trigger propagation
        to the block following n in q (see below).

    (b) If n is the exit block of some procedure p, i.e. $n = e_p$,
    find all pairs (m,u) such that m is a block following some call c
    to p, and PHI(c,u) = x, and for each such pair propagate (u,y) to m.

(c) If n is any other block in some procedure p, then, for each $m \in E_p^0 \{n\}$, propagate $(x, f_{(n,m)}(y))$ to m.

3. Repeat step 2 till WORK = $\emptyset$. When this happens, PHI represents the desired ϕ functions, computed only for "relevant" data values, from which the x solution can be readily computed as follows:

$$x_n = \bigwedge_{a \in L} PHI(n,a), \text{ for each } n \in N^*.$$

Step 3 thus implies that in the implementation we have sketched separate analysis to compute the x solution is unnecessary.

We omit analysis of the above algorithm, which in many ways would resemble an analysis of the abstract approach. However, so as not to avoid the issue of the correctness of our algorithm, we outline a proof of its total correctness, details of which can be readily filled in by the reader. The proof consists of several steps:

I. The algorithm terminates if L is finite, since each element (n,x) of $N^* \times L$ (which is a finite set) is added to WORK only a finite number of times, because the values assumed by PHI(n,x) upon successive insertions constitute a strictly decreasing sequence in L, which must of course be finite.

II. We claim that for each $n \in N^*$,

(1) $$x_n \leq \bigwedge_{a \in L} PHI(n,a) \quad .$$

To prove this claim, we show, using induction on the sequence of steps executed by the algorithm, that at the end of the i-th step, $x_n \leq \bigwedge_{a \in L} PHI^i(n,a)$, for each $n \in N^*$, $a \in L$, where PHI^i denotes the value of PHI at the end of the i-th step. In executing the i-th

step, we propagate some pair $(a,b) \in L \times L$ to some $n \in N^*$. By examining all possible cases, it is easy to show, using the induction hypothesis, that $x_n \leq b$, from which (1) follows immediately.

III. In order to prove the converse inequality, it is sufficient, by Theorem 3.4, to show that for each $n \in N^*$ and $q \in IVP(r_1,n)$,

$f_q(0) \geq \bigwedge\limits_{a \in L} PHI(n,a)$. To do this, we first need the following assertion:

(*) Let p be a procedure, $n \in N_p$ and $a \in L$ for which $PHI(n,a)$ has been computed by our algorithm. Then, for each path $q \in IVP_0(r_p,n)$,

$f_q(a) \geq PHI(n,a)$.

<u>Proof</u>: We proceed by induction on the length of q. This is trivial if the length = 0. Suppose that it is true for all p, n, a and q with length less than some $k > 0$, and let $q \in IVP_0(r_p,n)$ be of length k. Write $q = \hat{q}||(m,n)$ and observe that either $(m,n) \in E^0$, in which case

$$f_q(a) = f_{(m,n)}(f_{\hat{q}}(a)) \geq f_{(m,n)}(PHI(m,a)) \geq PHI(n,a)$$

(the last inequality follows from the structure of our algorithm), or (m,n) is a return edge, in which case q can be written as $\hat{q}_1||(c,r_{p'})||\hat{q}_2||(m,n)$, where $\hat{q}_1 \in IVP_0(r_p,c)$, $\hat{q}_2 \in IVP_0(r_{p'},m)$, and we have

$$f_q(a) = f_{\hat{q}_2}(f_{\hat{q}_1}(a)) \geq f_{\hat{q}_2}(PHI(c,a)) \geq PHI(m,PHI(c,a)) \geq PHI(n,a) .$$

IV. Now let q be any path in $IVP(r_1,n)$. Decompose q as in (3.1) $q = q_1||(c_1,r_{p_2})||\cdots||(c_j,r_{p_{j+1}})||q_{j+1}$. Then, using the monotonicity of F, we have

$$f_{q_1}(0) \geq PHI(c_1,0) = a_1$$

$$f_{q_2}(f_{q_1}(0)) \geq f_{q_2}(a_1) \geq PHI(c_2,a_1) = a_2$$

(this is because our algorithm will propagate (a_1,a_1) to r_{p_2}, so that $PHI(c_2,a_1)$ will eventually have been computed.) Continuing in this manner, we obtain $f_q(0) \geq PHI(n,a_j)$, which proves III. This completes the proof of the total correctness of our algorithm.

Example 4: Consider Example 1 given above. The steps taken by our iterative algorithm are summarized in the following table (where, for notational convenience, we represent PHI as a set of triplets, so that it contains (a,b,c) iff $PHI(a,b) = c$):

Propagate	from	to	entries added to PHI	WORK
	initially		$(r_1,0,0)$	$\{(r_1,0)\}$
$(0,1)$	r_1	c_1	$(c_1,0,1)$	$\{(c_1,0)\}$
$(1,1)$	c_1	r_2	$(r_2,1,1)$	$\{(r_2,1)\}$
$(1,0)$	r_2	c_2	$(c_2,1,0)$	$\{(c_2,1)\}$
$(1,1)$	r_2	e_2	$(e_2,1,1)$	$\{(c_2,1),(e_2,1)\}$
$(0,0)$	c_2	r_2	$(r_2,0,0)$	$\{(e_2,1),(r_2,0)\}$
$(0,1)$	e_2	n_1	$(n_1,0,1)$	$\{(r_2,0),(n_1,0)\}$
$(0,0)$	r_2	c_2	$(c_2,0,0)$	$\{(n_1,0),(c_2,0)\}$
$(0,0)$	r_2	e_2	$(e_2,0,0)$	$\{(n_1,0),(c_2,0),(e_2,0)\}$
$(0,1)$	n_1	e_1	$(e_1,0,1)$	$\{(c_2,0),(e_2,0),(e_1,0)\}$
$(0,0)$	c_2	n_2	$(n_2,0,0)$	$\{(e_2,0),(e_1,0),(n_2,0)\}$
$(1,0)$	e_2	n_2	$(n_2,1,0)$	$\{(e_1,0),(n_2,0),(n_2,1)\}$
$(0,0)$	e_2	n_2	–	$\{(e_1,0),(n_2,0),(n_2,1)\}$
–	e_1	–	–	$\{(n_2,0),(n_2,1)\}$
$(0,1)$	n_2	e_2	–	$\{(n_2,1)\}$
$(1,1)$	n_2	e_2	–	$\emptyset$

Finally we compute the x solution of Equations (3.2, 3.3) in step 3 of our iterative algorithm as follows:

$$x_{r_1} = \text{PHI}(r_1,0) = 0$$

$$x_{c_1} = \text{PHI}(c_1,0) = 1$$

$$x_{n_1} = \text{PHI}(n_1,0) = 1$$

$$x_{e_1} = \text{PHI}(e_1,0) = 1$$

$$x_{r_2} = \text{PHI}(r_2,0) \wedge \text{PHI}(r_2,1) = 0$$

$$x_{c_2} = \text{PHI}(c_2,0) \wedge \text{PHI}(c_2,1) = 0$$

$$x_{n_2} = \text{PHI}(n_2,0) \wedge \text{PHI}(n_2,1) = 0$$

$$x_{e_2} = \text{PHI}(e_2,0) \wedge \text{PHI}(e_2,1) = 0$$

4.   The call-string approach to inter-procedural analysis

     We now describe a second approach to inter-procedural analysis.
This approach views procedure calls and returns in much the same
way as any other transfer of control, but takes care to avoid propagation along non-interprocedurally valid paths. This is achieved by
tagging propagated data with an encoded history of procedure calls
along which that data has propagated. This contrasts with the idea
of tagging it by the lattice value attained on entrance to the most
recent procedure, as in the functional approach. In our second
approach, this 'propagation history' is updated whenever a call or a
return is encountered during propagation. This makes inter-
procedural flow explicit and increases the accuracy of propagated
information. Moreover, by passing to appropriate but simpler
encodings of the call history, we are able to derive approximate,
under-estimated information for any data-flow analysis, which should
nevertheless remain more accurate than that derived by ignoring
all inter-procedural constraints on the propagation. The fact that
this second approach allows us to perform approximate data-flow
analysis even in cases in which convergence of a full analysis is not
ensured or when the space requirements of a full analysis is prohibi-
tive, gives this second approach real advantages.

     We will first describe our second approach in a somewhat
abstract manner. We will then suggest several modifications which
yield relatively efficient convergent algorithms for many important
cases.

     As before, we suppose that we are given an interprocedural flow
graph G, but this time we make an explicit use of the second

representation $G^* = (N^*, E^*, r_1)$ of G. I.e., we do blend all procedures in G into one flow graph, but distinguish between intra-
procedural and inter-procedural edges.

Definition: A call string γ is a tuple of call blocks $c_1, c_2, \ldots, c_j$
in N^* for which there exists an execution path $q \in IVP(r_1, n)$,
terminating at some $n \in N^*$, such that the decomposition (3.1) of q
has the form $q_1 || (c_1, r_{p_2}) || q_2 \ldots || (c_j, r_{p_{j+1}}) || q_{j+1}$ where
$q_1 \in IVP_o(r_{p_1}, c_1)$ for each $1 \leq j$ and $q_{j+1} \in IVP_o(r_{p_{j+1}}, n)$. To show
the relation between q and γ we introduce a map CM such that
$CM(q) = \gamma$. By the uniqueness of the decomposition (3.1) (cf.
Lemma 3.1) this map is single-valued. γ can be thought of as the
contents of a stack containing the locations of all call instructions which have not yet been completed, in an implementation that
uses such a device.

Let Γ denote the space of all call strings γ corresponding
(in the above sense) to interprocedurally valid paths in G^*. Note
that is G^* is non-recursive, then Γ is finite; otherwise Γ will be
infinite, and as we shall soon see, this can cause difficulties for
our approach.

Let (L, F) be the data-flow framework under consideration. We
define a new framework (L^*, F^*), which reflects the inter-procedural
constraints in G^* in an implicit manner, as follows:

$L^* = L^\Gamma$, i.e. L^* is the space of all maps from Γ into L. Since
we assume that L contains a largest "undefined" element Ω, we can
identify L^* with the space of all partially defined maps from Γ into
$L - \{\Omega\}$. If Γ is finite, then the representation of L^* as a space
of partially defined maps is certainly more efficient, but for

abstract purposes the first representation is more convenient.

If $\xi \in L^*$ and $\gamma \in \Gamma$, then heuristically $\xi(\gamma)$ denotes that part of the propagated data which has been propagated along execution paths in $CM^{-1}\{\gamma\}$.

If we define a meet operation in L^* as a pointwise meet on Γ, i.e.- if for $\xi_1, \xi_2 \in L^*$, $\gamma \in \Gamma$, we define $(\xi_1 \wedge \xi_2)(\gamma) = \xi_1(\gamma) \wedge \xi_2(\gamma)$, then L^* becomes a semilattice. The smallest element in L^* is 0^*, where $0^*(\gamma) = 0$ for each $\gamma \in \Gamma$. The largest element in L^* is Ω^*, where $\Omega^*(\gamma) = \Omega$ for each $\gamma \in \Gamma$. Note that unless Γ is finite L^* need not be bounded. However, if $\xi_1 \geq \xi_2 \geq \ldots \geq \xi_n \geq \ldots$ is an infinite decreasing chain in L^*, its limit is well defined and can be computed as follows: For each $\gamma \in \Gamma$, the chain $\xi_1(\gamma) \geq \xi_2(\gamma) \geq \ldots$ must be finite (since L is bounded). Define $(\lim \xi_n)(\gamma)$ as the final value of that chain. Obviously $\lim_n \xi_n = \bigwedge_n \xi_n$ and in the same manner it can be shown that $\bigwedge_n \xi_n$ exists for any sequence $\{\xi_i\}_{i \geq 1}$ in L^*.

In order to describe F^* we first need to define a certain operation in Γ.

Definition: $\circ : \Gamma \times E^* \to \Gamma$ is a partially defined binary operation such that for each $\gamma \in \Gamma$ and $(m,n) \in E^*$ such that $CM^{-1}\{\gamma\} \cap IVP(r_1,m) \neq \emptyset$ we have

$$\gamma \circ (m,n) = \begin{cases} \gamma & \text{if } (m,n) \in E^O \\ \gamma||[m] & \text{if } (m,n) \text{ is a call edge in } E^1 \\ & \text{(i.e. if } m \text{ is a call block)} \\ \gamma(1:\#\gamma-1) & \text{(i.e. } \gamma \text{ without its last component)} \\ & \text{if } (m,n) \text{ is a return edge in } E^1 \text{ such} \\ & \text{that } \gamma(\#\gamma) \text{ is its corresponding call edge} \end{cases}$$

in all other cases, $\gamma \circ (m,n)$ is undefined.

The following lemma can be proved in an obvious and straightforward way.

Lemma 4.1: Let $\gamma \in \Gamma$, $(m,n) \in E^*$, $q \in IVP(r_1,m)$ such that $CM(q) = \gamma$. Then $\gamma_1 = \gamma \circ (m,n)$ is defined iff $q_1 = q||(m,n)$ is in $IVP(r_1,n)$, in which case $CM(q_1) = \gamma_1$.

The operation $\circ$ defines the manner in which call strings are updated as data is propagated along an edge of the flow graph. Loosely put, the above lemma states that path incrementation is transformed into $\circ$ by the "homomorphism" CM.

Next, let $(m,n) \in E^*$, and let $f_{(m,n)} \in F$ be the data-propagation map associated with (m,n). Note that by our assumptions $f_{(m,n)} = id_L$ if $(m,n) \in E^1$, since in these cases m is a block containing only a jump which in itself does not affect data attributes. Define $f^*_{(m,n)}: L^* \to L^*$ as follows: For each $\xi \in L^*$, $\gamma \in \Gamma$,

$$f^*_{(m,n)}(\xi)(\gamma) = \begin{cases} f_{(m,n)}(\xi(\gamma_1)) & \text{if there exists (necessarily a unique) } \gamma_1 \text{ such that } \gamma_1 \circ (m,n) = \gamma \\ \Omega & \text{otherwise} \end{cases}$$

The intuitive interpretation of this formula is as follows: $f^*_{(m,n)}(\xi)$ represents information at the start of n which is obtained by propagation of the information ξ, known at the start of m, along the edge (m,n). For each $\gamma_1 \in \Gamma$ for which $\xi(\gamma_1)$ is defined, we propagate $\xi(\gamma_1)$, the γ_1-selected data available at the start of m, to the start of n in standard intra-procedural fashion (that is, using $f_{(m,n)}$). However, this propagated data is now associated not with γ_1 but with $\gamma_1 \circ (m,n)$, which "tags" the set of paths obtained by concatenating (m,n) to all paths which are "tagged" by

γ_1, which lead to m, and along which $\xi(\gamma_1)$ has been propagated. If $\gamma_1 \circ (m,n)$ is undefined, then, by Lemma 4.1, $\xi(\gamma_1)$ should not be propagated through (m,n) since no path which leads to m and is tagged by γ_1 can be concatenated with (m,n) in a inter-procedurally valid manner. In this case, we simply discard $f_{(m,n)}(\xi(\gamma_1))$ as is indicated by the above formula.

F* is now defined as the smallest subset of maps acting in L* which contains $\{f^*_{(m,n)} : (m,n) \in E^*\}$ and the identity map in L* and which is closed under functional composition and meet.

Lemma 4.2: (a) If F is monotone in L, then F* is monotone in L*.

(b) If F is distributive in L, then F* is distributive in L*.

(c) If F is distributive in L, then for each $(m,n) \in E$, $f^*_{(m,n)}$ is continuous in L*, that is, $f^*_{(m,n)}(\bigwedge_k \xi_k) = \bigwedge_k f^*_{(m,n)}(\xi_k)$, for each collection $\{\xi_k\}_{k \geq 1} \subseteq L^*$.

Proof: It is easily seen that it is sufficient to prove (a) or (b) for the set $\{f^*_{(m,n)} : (m,n) \in E^*\}$, and this is straightforward from the definitions.

To prove (c), note that for each $\gamma \in \Gamma$ for which there exists $\gamma_1 \in \Gamma$ such that $\gamma_1 \circ (m,n) = \gamma$ we have

$$f^*_{(m,n)}(\bigwedge_{k \geq 1} \xi_k)(\gamma) = f_{(m,n)}[\bigwedge_{k \geq 1} \xi_k(\gamma_1)]$$

But since L is bounded, there exists $k_o(\gamma_1)$ such that the last expression equals $f_{(m,n)}[\bigwedge_{1 \leq k \leq k_o(\gamma_1)} \xi_k(\gamma_1)]$, which in turn, by the distributivity of $f_{(m,n)}$, equals

$$\bigwedge_{1 \leq k \leq k_o(\gamma_1)} f_{(m,n)}(\xi_k(\gamma_1))$$

$$= \bigwedge_{1 \leq k \leq k_o(\gamma_1)} f^*_{(m,n)}(\xi_k)(\gamma) \geq (\bigwedge_{k \geq 1} f^*_{(m,n)}(\xi_k))(\gamma) \ .$$

Thus $f^*_{(m,n)}(\bigwedge_{k \geq 1} \xi_k) \geq \bigwedge_{k \geq 1} f^*_{(m,n)}(\xi_k)$. The converse inequality is immediate from the monotonicity of $f^*_{(m,n)}$. $\hspace{2em}$ Q.E.D.

Remark: Note that inter-procedural, as distinct from intra-procedural, data-flow frameworks depend heavily on the flow-graph (Γ itself may vary from one flow graph to another). Thus, for example, there is no simple way to obtain F* directly from F without any reference to the flow graph. This will not create any problems in the sequel, and we argue that even in the intra-procedural case it is a better practice to regard data-flow frameworks as graph dependent.

We can now define a data-flow problem for G*, using the new framework (L*,F*), in which we seek the maximal fixed point solution of the following equations in L*:

$$x^*_{r_1} = \{(\lambda,0)\} \ , \text{ where } \lambda \text{ is the null call string}$$

(4.1)

$$x^*_n = \bigwedge_{(m,n) \in E^*} f^*_{(m,n)}(x^*_m), \quad n \in N^* - \{r_1\}$$

We can show the existence of a solution to those equations in the following manner: Let $x^{*(0)}_{r_1} = \{(\lambda,0)\}$, $x^{*(0)}_n = \Omega^*$ for all $n \in N^* - \{r_1\}$. Then apply Equations (4.1) iteratively to obtain new approximations to the x*'s. Let $x^{*(i)}_n$ denote the i-th approximation computed in this manner.

Since $x_n^{*(0)} \geq x_n^{*(1)}$ for all $n \in N^*$, it follows inductively, from the monotonicity of $f_{(m,n)}^*$ for each $(m,n) \in E^*$, that $x_n^{*(i)} \geq x_n^{*(i+1)}$ for all $i \geq 0$, $n \in N^*$. Thus, for each $n \in N^*$, $\{x_n^{*(i)}\}_{i \geq 0}$ is a decreasing chain in L^*, having a limit, and we define $x_n^* = \lim_i x_n^{*(i)}$. It is rather straightforward to show that $\{x_n^*\}_{n \in N^*}$ is indeed a solution to (4.1) and that in fact it is the maximal fixed point solution of (4.1).

Having defined this solution, we will want to convert its values to values in L, because L^* has been introduced only as an auxiliary semilattice, and our aim is really to obtain data in L for each basic block. Since there is no longer a need to split the data at node n into parts depending on the interprocedural flow leading to n, we can combine these parts together, i.e. take their meet. For each $n \in N^*$, we can then simply define

$$(4.2) \qquad\qquad x_n' = \bigwedge_{\gamma \in \Gamma} x_n^*(\gamma)$$

In justifying the approach that we have just outlined our first step is to prove that x_n' coincides with the meet over all interprocedurally valid paths solution y_n defined at the previous section. This can be shown as follows:

Definition: Let $\text{path}_{G^*}(r_1, n)$ denote the set of all execution paths (whether interprocedurally valid or not) leading from r_1 to $n \in N^*$. For each $p = (r_1, s_2, \ldots, s_k, n) \in \text{path}_{G^*}(r_1, n)$ define $f_p^* = f_{(s_k, n)}^* \circ f_{(a_{k-1}, s_k)}^* \cdots \circ f_{(r_1, s_2)}^*$. For each $n \in N^*$ define $y_n^* = \bigwedge \{f_p^*(x_{r_1}^*) : p \in \text{path}_{G^*}(r_1, n)\}$.

Since $\text{path}_{G^*}(r_1, n)$ is at most countable, this (possibly infinite) meet in L^* is well-defined.

Theorem 4.3: If (L,F) is a distributive data-flow framework then, for each $n \in N^*$, $x_n^* = y_n^*$.

Proof. (Which is quite similar to the proof of an analagous theorem of Kildall for a bounded semilattice [KI]):

(a) Let $n \in N^*$ and $p \equiv (r_1, s_2, \ldots, s_k, n) \in \text{path}_{G^*}(r_1, n)$. By (4.1) we have

$$x_{s_2}^* \leq f^*_{(r_1, s_2)}(x_{r_1}^*)$$

$$x_{s_3}^* \leq f^*_{(s_2, s_3)}(x_{s_2}^*)$$

$$\cdot$$
$$\cdot$$
$$\cdot$$

$$x_n^* \leq f^*_{(s_k, n)}(x_{s_k}^*)$$

Combining all these inequalities, and using the monotonicity of the f^*'s we obtain $x_n^* \leq f_p^*(x_{r_1}^*)$, and therefore $x_n^* \leq y_n^*$.

(b) Conversely, we will prove by induction on i that

$$x_n^{*(i)} \geq y_n^* \text{ for all } i \geq 0, \ n \in N^* \ .$$

Indeed, let $i=0$. If $n \neq r_1$ then $x_n^{*(0)} = \Omega^* \geq y_n^*$. On the other hand, the null execution path $p_0 \in \text{path}_{G^*}(r_1, r_1)$, so that $y_{r_1}^* \leq f_{p_0}^*(x_{r_1}^*) = x_{r_1}^* = x_{r_1}^{*(0)}$. Thus the assertion is true for $i=0$. Suppose that it is true for some $i \geq 0$. Then $x_{r_1}^{*(i+1)} = x_{r_1}^{*(i)} \geq y_{r_1}^*$, and for each $n \in N^* - \{r_1\}$ we have

$$x_n^{*(i+1)} = \bigwedge_{(m,n) \in E^*} f^*_{(m,n)}(x_m^{*(i)}) \geq \bigwedge_{(m,n) \in E^*} f^*_{(m,n)}(y_m^*)$$

by the induction hypothesis. We now need the following

Lemma 4.4: For each $(m,n) \in E^*$, $f^*_{(m,n)}(y_m^*) \geq y_n^*$.

<u>Proof</u>: Since $f^*_{(m,n)}$ is distributive and continuous on L^* (Lemma 4.2), we have

$$f^*_{(m,n)}(y^*_m) = f^*_{(m,n)}(\bigwedge \{f^*_p(x^*_{r_1}) ;\ p \in \text{path}_{G^*}(r_1,m)\})$$

$$= \bigwedge \{f^*_{(m,n)}(f^*_p(x^*_{r_1})) :\ p \in \text{path}_{G^*}(r_1,m)\}$$

$$\geq \bigwedge \{f^*_q(x^*_{r_1}) :\ q \in \text{path}_{G^*}(r_1,n)\} = y^*_n$$

$$\text{Q.E.D.}$$

Now returning to Theorem 4.3 it follows by Lemma 4.4 that
$x^{*(i+1)}_n \geq \bigwedge_{(m,n) \in E^*} y^*_n = y^*_n$ (each $n \in N^*$ is assumed to have pre-
decessors). Hence assertion (b) is established, and it follows that
for each $n \in N^*$ $x^*_n = \lim_i x^{*(i)}_n = \bigwedge_{i \geq 1} x^{*(i)}_n \geq y^*_n$, so that $x^*_n = y^*_n$.

$$\text{Q.E.D.}$$

<u>Lemma 4.5</u>: Let $n \in N^*$, $p = (r_1, s_2, \ldots, s_k, n) \in \text{path}_{G^*}(r_1, n)$ and
$\gamma \in \Gamma$. Then $f^*_p(x^*_{r_1})(\gamma)$ is defined iff $p \in \text{IVP}(r_1, n)$ and $CM(p) = \gamma$.
If this is the case, then $f^*_p(x^*_{r_1})(\gamma) = f_p(0)$.

<u>Proof</u>: The proof is by induction on $\ell(p)$, the length of p (i.e. the
number of edges in p). If p is the null path, then n must be equal
to r_1. Moreover, $CM(p) = \lambda$, $p \in \text{IVP}(r_1, r_1)$ and $f^*_p(x^*_{r_1}) = x^*_{p_1}$ is
defined only at λ and equals $0 = f_p(0)$. Thus our assertion is true
if $\ell(p) = 0$.

Suppose that this assertion is true for all $n \in N^*$ and
$p \in \text{path}_{G^*}(r_1, n)$ such that $\ell(p) < \lambda$. Let $n \in N^*$ and $p =
(r_1, s_2, \ldots, s_k, n)$ be a path of length k in $\text{path}_{G^*}(r_1, n)$. Let
$p_1 = (r_1, s_2, \ldots, s_k)$. By definition, for each $\gamma \in \Gamma$ we have

$$f_p^*(x_{r_1}^*)(\gamma) = f_{(s_k,n)}^*[f_{p_1}^*(x_{r_1}^*)](\gamma)$$

$$= \begin{cases} f_{(s_k,n)}[f_{p_1}^*(x_{r_1}^*)(\gamma_1)] & \text{if there exists} \\ & \gamma_1 \in \Gamma \text{ such that} \\ & \gamma_1 \circ (s,n) = \gamma \\ & k \\ \Omega & \text{otherwise} \end{cases}$$

Thus $f_p^*(x_{r_1}^*)(\gamma)$ is defined iff there exists $\gamma_1 \in \Gamma$ such that $\gamma_1 \circ (m,n) = \gamma$ and $f_{p_r}^*(x_{r_1}^*)(\gamma_1)$ is defined. By our inductive hypothesis, this is the case iff $p_1 \in \text{IVP}(r_1,s_k)$, $\text{CM}(p_1) = \gamma_1$ and $\gamma_1 \circ (s_k,n) = \gamma$. By Lemma 4.1, these last conditions are equivalent to $p \in \text{IVP}(r_1,n)$ and $\text{CM}(p) = \gamma$.

If this is the case, then again, by our inductive hypothesis, $f_{p_1}^*(x_{r_1}^*)(\gamma_1) = f_{p_1}(0)$ and so

$$f_p^*(x_{r_1}^*)(\gamma) = f_{(s_k,n)}[f_{p_1}(0)] = f_p(0)$$

Q.E.D.

Now we can prove the main result of this section:

Theorem 4.6: For each $n \in N^*$, $x_n' = y_n$.

Proof: Let $\gamma \in \Gamma$. By Theorem 4.3,

$$x_n^*(\gamma) = \{f_p^*(x_{r_1}^*)(\gamma): p \in \text{path}_{G^*}(r_1,n)\}$$

and by Lemma 4.5

$$= \bigwedge \{f_p(0): p \in \text{IVP}(r_1,n) \text{ such that } \text{CM}(p) = \gamma\}.$$

Thus, by (4.2),

$$x_n' = \bigwedge_{\gamma \in \Gamma} x_n^*(\gamma) = \bigwedge \{f_p(0): p \in \text{IVP}(r_1,n)\} = y_n$$

Q.E.D.

Corollary 4.7: If the flow graph G^* is non-recursive then the iterative solution of Equations (4.1) that we have described will converge and yield the desired meet over all interprocedurally valid paths solution of these equations.

Proof: Convergence is assured since Γ is finite and hence L^* is bounded. Thus (L^*,F^*) is a distributive data-flow framework and by standard arguments the iterative solution of (4.1) must converge (cf. [KI] or [HE]). Therefore, Theorem 4.6 implies that the limiting solution coincides with the meet over all paths solution.

Q.E.D.

The call-strings approach is of questionable feasibility if Γ is infinite, i.e. if G^* contains recursive procedures. Moreover, just as for the functional approach, it is rather hopeless to convert the call strings approach into an effective algorithm for handling the most general cases of certain data-flow problems such as constant propagation. However, as we shall see in the following section, a fairly practical variant of the call strings approach can be devised for data-flow frameworks with a finite semilattice L.

5. Data-flow analyses using a finite semilattice

Let (L,F) be a distributive data-flow framework such that L is
finite. As we have seen, the functional approach described in
Section 3 converges for such a framework. We will show in this
section that it is also possible to construct a call-strings algorithm which converges for these frameworks. As noted in the previous
section, convergence is ensured if Γ is finite. The idea behind our
modified approach is to replace Γ by some finite subset Γ_0 and allow
propagation only through inter-procedurally valid paths which are
mapped into elements of Γ_0. Such an approach is not generally
feasible since it can lead to an over-estimated (and unsafe) solution,
since it does not trace information along all possible paths. However, using the finiteness of L, we will show that Γ_0 can be chosen
in such a way that no information gets lost and the algorithm comes
up with an acceptable solution.

We begin to describe our approach without fully specifying Γ_0.
Later we will show how Γ_0 should depend on L in order to guarantee
an acceptable solution.

Definitions: (a) Let Γ_0 be some finite subset of Γ with the property
that if $\gamma \in \Gamma_0$ and γ_1 is an initial subtuple of γ, then $\gamma_1 \in \Gamma_0$ too.
(b) For each $n \in N^*$, let $IVP'(r_1,n)$ denote the set of all
$q \in IVP(r_1,n)$ such that for each initial subpath q_1 of q (including q),
$CM(q_1) \in \Gamma_0$.

(c) We also modify the ∘ operation so that it acts in Γ_0 rather than in Γ, as follows: If $\gamma \in \Gamma_0$, $(m,n) \in E^*$ such that there exists $q \in IVP'(r_1,m)$ where $CM(q) = \gamma$, then

$$\gamma \circ (m,n) = \begin{cases} \gamma & \text{if } (m,n) \in E^0 \\ \gamma \,||\, [m] & \text{if } (m,n) \text{ is a call edge in } E^1 \text{ and} \\ & \qquad \gamma \,||\, [m] \in \Gamma_0 \\ \gamma(1: \#\gamma-1) & \text{if } (m,n) \text{ is a return edge in } E^1 \text{ and} \\ & \qquad \gamma(\#\gamma) \text{ is the call block preceding } n \\ \text{undefined} & \text{in all other cases} \end{cases}$$

The only difference between this definition of ∘ and the previous one is that it will not add a call block m to a call string γ unless the resulting string is in Γ_0. When this is not the case, information tagged by γ will be lost when propagating through (m,n), unless it is also tagged by some other call string to which m can be concatenated. The following lemma is analogous to Lemma 4.1:

Lemma 5.1: Let $\gamma \in \Gamma_0$, $(m,n) \in E^*$, $q \in IVP'(r_1,m)$ such that $CM(q) = \gamma$. Then $\gamma_1 = \gamma$ (m,n) is defined iff $q_1 = q \,||\, (m,n)$ is in $IVP'(r_1,n)$, in which case $CM(q_1) = \gamma_1$.

We now define a data-flow framework (L^*, F^*) in much the same way as in Section 4, but replace Γ by Γ_0. This leads to a bounded semilattice $L^* = L^{\Gamma_0}$ and to a distributive data-flow framework (L^*, F^*).

Hence, Equations (4.1) come to be effectively solvable by any standard iterative algorithm which yields their maximal fixed point solution. To this solution we will want to apply the following final calculation, which is a variant of (4.2):

(5.1)
$$x_n'' = \bigwedge_{\gamma \in \Gamma_o} x_n^*(\ )$$

Careful scrutiny of the analysis of the previous section reveals that the only place where the nature of Γ_o and the operation $\circ$ are referred to is in Lemma 4.1, and it is easily seen that if we replace Γ and $\circ$ by Γ_o and the modified $\circ$, throughout the previous analysis, and also replace $IVP(r_1,n)$ by $IVP'(r_1,n)$ for all $n \in N^*$, then by proofs completely analogous to those presented in Section 4 (but with one notable difference, i.e. that there is now no need to worry about continuity of F^* or infinite meets in L^*, since L^* is now known to be bounded), we obtain the following:

Theorem 5.2: For each $n \in N^*$

$$x_n'' = y_n'' \equiv \bigwedge \{f_p(0): p \in IVP'(r_1,n)\}$$

Up to this point, our suggested modifications have been quite general and do not impose any particular requirements upon L or upon Γ_o. On the other hand, Theorem 5.2 implies that x_n'' is an over-estimated solution, and as such is useless for purposes of our analysis, as it can yield unsafe information (e.g. may suggest that an expression is available whereas it may actually be unavailable), unless we can show that x_n'' coincides with the meet over all inter-procedurally valid paths solution of the attribute-propagation equations which concern us. As will be shown below, this is indeed the case if L is finite.

Definition: Let $M \geq 0$ be an integer. Define Γ_M as the (finite) set of all call strings whose length does not exceed M. Γ_M

obviously satisfies the conditions of part (a) of the previous definition.

Lemma 5.3: Let (L,F) be a data-flow framework with a finite semi-lattice, and let $M = K(|L|+1)^2$, where K is the number of call blocks in the program being analyzed and $|L|$ is the cardinality of L. Let $\Gamma_0 = \Gamma_M$. Then, for each $n \in N^*$ and each execution path $q \in IVP(r_1,n)$ there exists another path $q' \in IVP'(r_1,n)$ such that $f_q(0) = f_{q'}(0)$.

Proof. By induction on the length of q. If the length is 0 then $n=r_1$ and q is the null execution path, which belongs to both $IVP(r_1,r_1)$ and $IVP'(r_1,r_1)$, so that our assertion is obviously true in this case.

Suppose that the lemma is true for all paths whose length is less than some $k \geq 1$, and let $n \in N^*$, $q \in IVP(r_1,n)$ be a path of length k. If $q \in IVP'(r_1,n)$ then there is nothing to prove, so assume that this is not the case, and let q_0 be the shortest initial subpath of q such that $CM(q_0) \notin \Gamma_0$. Then q_0 can be decomposed according to (3.1) as follows:

$$q_0 = q_1 || (c_1, r_{p_2}) || q_2 || \cdots || (c_j, r_{p_{j+1}}) || q_{j+1}$$

Hence $j > M$. Next, consider the sequence $\{(c_i, \alpha_i, \beta_i)\}_{i=1}^{j}$, where, for each $i \leq j$, $\alpha_i = f_{q_i} \circ f_{q_{i-1}} \cdots \circ f_{q_1}(0)$, and β_i is either Ω if the call at c_i is not completed in q (this call is certainly not completed in q_0), or $f_{\hat{q}_i}(0)$ if the call at c_i is completed in q, and $\hat{q}_i$ is the initial subpath of q ending at the return which completes the call. Thus, for each call, the sequence records the

calling block, the value propagated along this path until the call, and the value propagated until the corresponding return, if it materializes. The number of distinct elements of such a sequence is at most $K(|L|+1)^2 = M$ (we do not count Ω as an element of L; if we did, then the bound can be reduced to $K|L|^2$). Since $j > M$, this sequence must contain at least two identical components $(c_{i_1}, \alpha_{i_1}, \beta_{i_1})$ and $(c_{i_2}, \alpha_{i_2}, \beta_{i_2})$, where $i_1 < i_2 \leq j$.

Now, if $\beta_{i_1} = \beta_{i_2} = \Omega$, then neither of the calls c_{i_1}, c_{i_2} is completed in q. If we rewrite

$$q = q_1' || (c_{i_1}, r_{p_{i+1}}) || q_2' || (c_{i_2}, r_{p_{i+1}}) || q_3'$$

then it is easily seen that the shorter path $\hat{q} = q_1' || (c_{i_1}, r_{p_{i+1}}) || q_3'$

is also in $IVP(r_1, n)$. Moreover

$$\alpha_{i_1} = f_{q_1'}(0) = \alpha_{i_2} = f_{q_2'} \circ f_{q_1'}(0)$$

so that

$$f_q(0) = f_{q_3'} \circ f_{q_2'} \circ f_{q_1'}(0) = f_{q_3'} \circ f_{q_1'}(0) = f_{\hat{q}}(0).$$

By our induction hypothesis there exists $\hat{q}' \in IVP'(r_1, n)$ such that $f_{\hat{q}'}(0) = f_{\hat{q}}(0) = f_q(0)$, which proves the lemma for q.

On the other hand, if $\beta_{i_1} = \beta_{i_2} \neq \Omega$, then it follows that both calls c_{i_1} and c_{i_2} are completed in q, with c_{i_2} necessarily completed first. Thus we can write

$$q = q_1' || (c_{i_1}, r_{p_{i+1}}) || q_2' || (c_{i_2}, r_{p_{i+1}}) || q_3' || (e_{p_{i+1}}, n_{i_2}) || q_4' ||$$

$$(e_{p_{i+1}}, n_{i_1}) || q_5'$$

where $n_{1_1} = n_{1_2}$ is the block immediately following c_{1_1}. Again it follows that $\hat{q} = q_1' \,||\, (c_{1_1}, r_{p_{i+1}^1}) \,||\, q_3' \,||\, (e_{p_{i+1}^1}, n_{1_1}) \,||\, q_5'$ is in

IVP (r_1, n). Moreover

$$\alpha_{i_1} = f_{q_1'}(0) = \alpha_{i_2} = f_{q_2'} \circ f_{q_1'}(0)$$

$$\beta_{i_1} = f_{q_4'} \circ f_{q_3'} \circ f_{q_2'} \circ f_{q_1'}(0) = \beta_{i_2} = f_{q_3'} \circ f_{q_2'} \circ f_{q_1'}(0)$$

from which one easily obtains $f_q(0) = f_{\hat{q}}(0)$, and the proof can now continue exactly as before.

Q.E.D.

The main result of this section now follows immediately:

Theorem 5.4: Let (L,F) be a distributive data-flow framework with a finite semilattice L, and let $\Gamma_0 = \Gamma_M$, with M as defined above. Then, for each $n \in N^*$, $x_n'' = y_n$. That is, the modified algorithm described in the first pages of the present section yields a valid inter-procedural solution.

Proof: Since IVP'$(r_1, n) \subseteq$ IVP(r_1, n) we have $x_n'' \geq y_n$. On the other hand, let $q \in$ IVP(r_1, n). By Lemma 5.3 there exists $q' \in$ IVP'(r_1, n) such that $f_q(0) = f_{q'}(0) \geq \{f_p(0): p \in$ IVP'$(r_1, n)\} = x_n''$. Hence $y_n = \bigwedge \{f_q(0): q \in$ IVP$(r_1, n)\} \geq x_n''$.

Q.E.D.

Remark: Note that in Lemma 5.3 and Theorem 5.4 K can be replaced by the maximal number K' of distinct calls in any sequence of nested calls in the program being analyzed. In most cases this gives a significant improvement of the bound on M appearing in these two results.

We have now shown that finite data-flow frameworks are solvable by a modified call-strings approach. However, the size of Γ_o can be expected to be large enough to make this approach as impractical as the corresponding functional approach. But in several special cases we can reduce the size of Γ_o still further.

Definition: A data-flow framework (L,F) is called <u>decomposable</u> if there exists a finite set A and a collection of data-flow frameworks $\{(L_\alpha, F_\alpha)\}_{\alpha \in A}$, such that

(1) $L = \prod_{\alpha \in A} L_\alpha$, ordered in a pointwise manner induced by the individual orders in each L_α.

(2) $F \subseteq \bigoplus_{\alpha \in A} F$. That is, for each $f \in F$ there exists a collection $\{f^\alpha\}_{\alpha \in A}$ where $f^\alpha \in F$ for each $\alpha \in A$, such that for each $x = (x_\alpha)_{\alpha \in A} \in L$ we have

$$f(x) = (f^\alpha(x_\alpha))_{\alpha \in A}$$

In the cases covered by this definition we can split our data-flow framework into a finite number of "independent" frameworks, each inducing a separate data-flow problem, and obtain the solution to the original problem simply by grouping all the individual solutions together.

For example, the standard framework (L,F) for available expressions analysis is decomposable into subframeworks each of which is a framework for the availability of a single expression. Formally, let A be the set of all program expressions. For each $\alpha \in A$ let $L = \{0,1\}$ where 1 indicates that α is available and 0 that it is not. Then $\{0,1\}^A$ is isomorphic with L (which is more conveniently

represented as the power set of A). It is easily checked that each
f ε F can be decomposed as $\oplus_{\alpha \in A} f^{\alpha}$, where for each $\alpha \in A$ $f^{\alpha} \in F_{\alpha}$,
and is either the constant 0 if α can be killed by the propagation
step described by f, f^{α} is the constant 1 if α is unconditionally
generated by that propagation step, and is the identity map in all
other cases. The frameworks used for use-definition chaining and
live variables have analogous decompositions.

A straightforward modification of Lemma 5.3, applied to each
(L_{α}, F_{α}) separately yields the following improved result for decomposable frameworks:

<u>Theorem 5.5</u>: Let (L,F) be a decomposable distributive data-flow
framework with a finite semilattice. Define $M = K \cdot \max_{\alpha \in A}(|L_{\alpha}|+1)^2$
and let $\Gamma_o = \Gamma_M$. Then, for each n ε N*, $y_n'' = y_n$.

In the special case of available expressions analysis this is
certainly an improvement of Theorem 5.4, since it reduces the bound
on the length of permissible call-strings from $K \cdot O(4^{|A|})$ to 9K.
For this analysis we can do even better since available expression
analysis has the property appearing in the following definition.

<u>Definition</u>: A decomposable data-flow framework (L,F) is called
<u>1-related</u> if, for each $\alpha \in A$, F_{α} consists only of constant functions
and identity functions.

This property is characteristic of situations in which there
exists at most one point along each path which can affect the data
being propagated. Indeed, consider a framework having this property,
let $\alpha \in A$ and let $p = (s_1, s_2, \ldots, s_K)$ be an execution path. Let $j \leq k$
be the largest index such that $f^{\alpha}_{(s_{j-1}, s_j)}$ is a constant function.
Then clearly $f^{\alpha}_p = f^{\alpha}_{(s_{j-1}, s_j)}$ and is therefore also a constant. Hence

this case the effect of propagation in L_α through p is independent of the initial data and is determined by the edge (s_{j-1}, s_j) alone. If no such j exists, then $f_p = id|_{L_\alpha}$, in which case no point along p affects the final data.

Note also that since each F_α is assumed to be closed under functional meet, it follows that if (L,F) is 1-related then the only constant functions that F_α can contain are 0 (the smallest element in L_α) and 1 (the largest element). Hence we can assume, with no loss of generality, that L_α is the trivial lattice {0,1} for each $\alpha \in A$. All the classical data-flow analyses mentioned above have 1-related frameworks.

For frameworks having the 1-related property it is easy to replace an execution path q by a shorter subpath $\hat{q}$ such that $f_{\hat{q}}^\alpha(0) = f_q^\alpha(0)$ for some $\alpha \in A$. Indeed, to obtain such a $\hat{q}$ we have only to ensure that $\hat{q}$ is also inter-procedurally valid and that the last edge (s,s') in q for which $f_{(s,s')}$ is constant belongs to $\hat{q}$. This observation allows us to restrict the length of permissible call strings still further. The following can then be shown:

Theorem 5.6. Let (L,F) be a 1-related distributive data-flow framework. Put $\Gamma_0 = \Gamma_{3K}$. Then, for each $n \in N^*$, $x_n'' = y_n$.

The analysis developed in this section and the previous one can be modified to deal with non-distributive data-flow problems. In the non-distributive case, Theorems 4.6 and 5.2 only guarantee inequalities of the form $x_n' \leq y_n$ (resp. $x_n'' \leq y_n''$) for all $n \in N^*$. The arguments in this section show that under appropriate conditions

$y_n'' = y_n$ for each $n \in N^*$, so that assuming these conditions Theorems 5.4, 5.5, 5.6 all yield the inequalities $x_n'' \leq y_n$ for each $n \in N^*$. Thus, in the non-distributive case, our approach leads to an underestimated solution, as is the case for intra-procedural iterative algorithms for non-distributive frameworks (cf. [KU1]).

Example 5: We return to Example 1 studied in Section 3. Since available expressions analysis uses a 1-related framework, and since the flow graph appearing in that example satisfies $K = K' = 2$, we can take $\Gamma_0 = \Gamma_6$, and apply Kildall's iterative algorithm [KI] to solve Equations (4.1). The following table summarizes the steps which are then performed (for notational call strings are written without enclosing parenthesis):

propagate from	to	updated x* value	workpile of nodes from which further propagation is required
initially		$x_{r_1}^* = \{(\lambda,0)\}$	$\{r_1\}$
r_1	c_1	$x_{c_1}^* = \{(\lambda,1)\}$	$\{c_1\}$
c_1	r_2	$x_{r_2}^* = \{(c_1,1)\}$	$\{r_2\}$
r_2	c_2	$x_{c_2}^* = \{(c_1,0)\}$	$\{c_2\}$
r_2	e_2	$x_{e_2}^* = \{(c_1,1)\}$	$\{c_2,e_2\}$
c_2	r_2	$x_{r_2}^* = \{(c_1,1),(c_1c_2,0)\}$	$\{e_2,r_2\}$
e_2	n_2	$x_{n_2}^* = \Omega^*$(unchanged)	$\{r_2\}$
e_2	n_1	$x_{n_1}^* = \{(\lambda,1)\}$	$\{r_2,n_1\}$
r_2	c_2	$x_{c_2}^* = \{(c_1,0),(c_1c_2,0)\}$	$\{n_1,c_2\}$
r_2	e_2	$x_{e_2}^* = \{(c_1,1),(c_1c_2,0)\}$	$\{n_1,c_2,e_2\}$
n_1	e_1	$x_{e_1}^* = \{(\lambda,1)\}$	$\{c_2,e_2,e_1\}$
c_2	r_2	$x_{r_2}^* = \{(c_1,1),(c_1c_2,0),(c_1c_2c_2,0)\}$	$\{e_2,e_1,r_2\}$
e_2	n_2	$x_{n_2}^* = \{(c_1,0)\}$	$\{e_1,r_2,n_2\}$
e_2	n_1	—	$\{e_1,r_2,n_2\}$
e_1	—	—	$\{r_2,n_2\}$

The next steps of the algorithm update $x^*_{r_2}, x^*_{c_2}, x^*_{n_2}, x^*_{e_2}$ in similar fashion, adding new entries with increasingly longer call strings, up to a string $c_1 c_2 c_2 c_2 c_2 c_2$, but none of $x^*_{r_1}, x^*_{c_1}, x^*_{n_1}$ or $x^*_{e_1}$ is ever modified. Final x* values for the blocks appearing in our example are

$$x^*_{r_2} = x^*_{e_2} = \{(c_1,1),\ (c_1 c_2,0),\ (c_1 c_2 c_2,0)\ \cdots\ (c_1 c_2 c_2 c_2 c_2 c_2,0)\}$$

$$x^*_{c_2} = \{(c_1,0),\ (c_1 c_2,0),\ \cdots\ (c_1 c_2 c_2 c_2 c_2 c_2,0)\}$$

$$x^*_{n_2} = \{(c_1,0),\ (c_1 c_2,0),\ \cdots\ (c_1 c_2 c_2 c_2 c_2,0)\}\quad (\neq x^*_{c_2},\ \text{by the way})$$

An x" solution can now be easily computed, of course, this is identical to the solutions obtained by previous methods.

Note that in this example there was no need to maintain call strings of length up to 6 (length 2 would have sufficed). However, to derive correct information in the following example we need call strings in which one call appears three times.

Example 2:

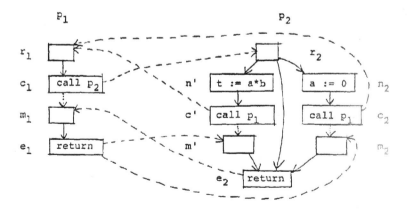

The shortest path showing that a*b is <u>not</u> available at m' is
$q = (r_1, c_1, r_2, n', c', r_1, c_1, r_2, n_2, c_2, r_1, c_1, r_2, e_2, m_1,$
$e_1, m_2, e_2, m_1, e_1, m')$, in which c_1 appears three times before
any of the calls in q is completed.

It is an interesting and challenging problem to find, for
a given flow graph, by some preliminary analysis, an optimal set
Γ_o of call strings needed to perform some particular interprocedural
data-flow analysis without losing information.

5.   An approximative call-string approach

In this section we present a modification of the call-string approach developed in Section 4, which yields a convergent algorithm for any data-flow analysis, even though this algorithm may in general fail to produce precisely the desired (meet over all inter-procedurally-valid paths) solution. However, the output of the algorithm to be presented will always be an underestimated (and hence safe) solution. This compromise which is useful even when L is finite, can make the call-string approach much more efficient. Moreover, if L is infinite, F is not bounded or does not admit compact representation then this modified approach is one of the very few ways to perfrom inter-procedural analysis that we know.

Three things should be kept in mind when evaluating any approximative approach to an interprocedural data-flow problem: (a) Even in intraprocedural analysis, a meet over all paths solution is itself an underestimation to the "true" run-time situation, since many of the static execution paths which enter into such an analysis may not be executable. (b) Many data-flow analyses whose semi-lattice L is not finite are also not distributive (cf. [KUl] and [SH]) so that even the intra-procedural iterative solution of the data-flow equations may underestimate the meet over all paths solu-tion, and, furthermore, (c) in non-distributive cases, the meet over all paths solution may not be calculable (cf. [HE] for details).

By analyzing the abstract approach presented in Section 4, we can easily see that the convergence (and efficiency) of the call strings approach depends primarily on Γ. Convergence can be ensured in general only if Γ is finite, and the smaller Γ is, the less complex the algorithm becomes. This observation motivates the

approach that we propose in this section, whose general outline is as follows.

Choose some finite (preferably rather small) set $\hat{\Gamma}$ which is closed under a binary operation * and has a left identity with respect to this operation. (In practice, we suggest that * be associative and non-commutative, but the general description given below will not assume this.) As in Section 4, let Γ denote the set of all call strings. Choose an "encoding" map σ which maps each call block to some element of $\hat{\Gamma}$. Using *, we can extend σ to Γ by putting $\sigma(\gamma) = \sigma(c_1) * \sigma(c_2) * \ldots * \sigma(c_j)$ (computed left-to-right) for each $\gamma = (c_1, c_2, \ldots, c_j) \in \Gamma$. We also define $\sigma(\lambda)$ to be w, the left-identity of $\hat{\Gamma}$.

Let (L,F) be any (not necessarily distributive) data-flow framework. We will define a modified data-flow framework (L^*, F^*) in essentially the same way as we did in Section 4, but with some differences reflecting the nature of the approximative approach, as detailed below.

L^* is defined as $L^{\hat{\Gamma}}$. All the observations made in Section 4 concerning L^* still apply, only now L^* is bounded since $\hat{\Gamma}$ has been assumed to be finite.

As before, in order to define F^*, we first define an updating operation between encoded call strings and edges in E^*. This updating operation is now more complex than that defined earlier, and in order to describe it we first introduce the following

Definition: For each procedure p in the program being analyzed, define $ECS(p) = \{\sigma(CM(q)): q \in IVP(r_1, r_p)\}$. This is the set of all encoded call strings which result from interprocedurally valid paths

reaching the entry of p.

These sets can be calculated by a rather simple preliminary analysis based upon the following set of equations (where *main* denotes the main program, which is assumed to be non-recursive):

$$ECS(main) = \{w\}$$

(6.1)

$$ECS(p) = \{\alpha * \sigma(c): c \text{ is a call to p from some procedure p' and}$$
$$\alpha \in ECS(p')\}, \qquad\qquad p \neq main$$

After initializing each ECS(p) to $\emptyset$, for all $p \neq main$, these equations can be solved iteratively in a fairly standard way. (The iterative solution will converge because $\hat{\Gamma}$ is finite.) It is a simple matter to prove that the iterative solution yields the sets ECS(p) defined above.

Using the sets ECS we now define the following objects: For each $n \in N^*$, a set of <u>inter-procedurally acceptable</u> paths leading from the main entry to n, denoted by $IAP(r_1,n)$; a modified set-valued map $\hat{CM}$ from $\bigcup_{n \in N^*} IAP(r_1,n)$ to $2^{\hat{\Gamma}}$, and a modified set-valued operation $\hat{o}: \hat{\Gamma} \times E^* \to 2^{\hat{\Gamma}}$. These recursive definitions are as follows:

(a) The null execution path q_0 is in $IAP(r_1,r_1)$ and $\hat{CM}(q_0) = \{w\}$.

(b) Let $n \in N^*$ and q be an execution path leading to n. Write $q = q_1 || (m,n)$. Then $q \in IAP(r_1,n)$ iff $q_1 \in IAP(r_1,m)$ and the set $A = \bigcup \{\alpha \, \hat{o}(m,n): \alpha \in \hat{CM}(q_1)\}$ is not empty, where, for each $\alpha \in \hat{CM}[IAP(r_1,m)]$ and $(m,n) \in E^*$ we define $\alpha \, \hat{o}(m,n)$ by

$$\alpha \, \hat{o}(m,n) = \begin{cases} \{\alpha\} & \text{if } (m,n) \in E^O \\ \{\alpha * \sigma(m)\} & \text{if } (m,n) \text{ is a call edge} \\ \{\beta \in ECS(p) \,|\, \beta * \sigma(c) = \alpha\} & \text{if } (m,n) \text{ is a return edge} \\ & \quad \text{corresponding to a call edge from a call block} \\ & \quad c \text{ in procedure p.} \end{cases}$$

In all cases we define $\hat{CM}(q)$ to be the set A introduced just above.

The intuitive meaning of these concepts can be explained as follows: Since we have decided to record the actual call string by a homomorphism CM of paths into a finite set $\hat{\Gamma}$, it is inevitable that we will also admit paths which are not in $IVP(r_1,n)$. Thus $IAP(r_1,n) \supseteq IVP(r_1,n)$, and will also contain paths which the encoding CM cannot distinguish from valid IVP paths. In particular, some returns not to their originating calls will have to be admitted.

An immediate consequence of the preceding definition, provable by induction on the length of the execution path q, is as follows·

Lemma 6.1: An execution path q is interprocedurally acceptable iff $\widehat{CM}(q) \neq \emptyset$.

Having defined IAP, $\widehat{CM}$, and $\hat{o}$, we next define F* in essentially the same manner as in Section 4. Specifically, for each $(m,n) \in E^*$ we define $f^*_{(m,n)}: L^* \to L^*$ as follows: For each $\xi \in L^*$, $\alpha \in \hat{\Gamma}$

$$f^*_{(m,n)}(\xi)(\alpha) = \bigwedge \{f_{(m,n)}(\xi(\alpha_1)): \alpha \in \alpha_1 \; \hat{o}(m,n)\}$$

where it is agreed that an empty meet yields Ω.

F* is now constructed from the functions $f^*_{(m,n)}$ exactly as before. The heuristic significance of this definition is the same as in Section 4, only now the "tag" updating which occurs when propagation takes place along an interprocedural edge involves less extensive and precise information. The modified updating operation that has just been defined can be both one-to-many and many-to-one, possibilities which are both reflected in the above formula. It is easy to verify that both monotonicity and distributivity are preserved as we pass from (L,F) to (L*,F*).

Next we associate with (L*,F*) the data-flow problem of determining the maximal fixed point solution of the equations

$$x^*_{r_1} = \{(w,0)\}$$

(6.2)

$$x^*_n = \bigwedge_{(m,n) \in E^*} f^*_{(m,n)}(x^*_m), \qquad n \in N^* - \{r_1\}$$

As previously, a solution of these equations can be obtained by standard iterative techniques. Once this solution has been obtained we make the following final calculation:

$$(6.3) \qquad \hat{x}_n = \bigwedge_{\alpha \in \hat{\Gamma}} x_n^*(\alpha)$$

The techniques of Section 4 can now be applied to analyze the procedure just described. Theorem 4.3 retains its validity, if re-stated as follows:

Theorem 6.2: (a) If (L,F) is distributive then, for each $n \in N^*$, $x_n^* = y_n^* \equiv \bigwedge \{f_p^*(x_{r_1}^*): p \in \text{path}_{G*}(r_1,n)\}$.

(b) If (L,F) is only monotone then, for each $n \in N^*$, $x_n^* \leq y_n^*$.

Instead of Lemma 4.5, the following variant applies:

Lemma 6.3: Let $n \in N^*$, $p \in \text{path}_{G*}(r_1,n)$ and $\alpha \in \hat{\Gamma}$. Then $f_p^*(x_{r_1}^*)(\alpha)$ is defined iff $\alpha \in \hat{CM}(p)$, in which case $f_p^*(x_{r_1}^*)(\alpha) = f_p(0)$.

Proof: By induction on the length of p. The assertion is obvious if p is the null execution path. Suppose that it is true for all paths with length $< k$ and let $p = (r_1, s_2, \ldots, s_k, n) \in \text{path}_{G*}(r_1,n)$ be a path of length k. Let $p_1 = (r_1, s_2, \ldots, s_k)$. Then for each $\alpha \in \hat{\Gamma}$ we have

$$f_p^*(x_{r_1}^*)(\alpha) = f_{(s_k,n)}^*[f_{p_1}^*(x_{r_1}^*)](\alpha) =$$

$$\bigwedge \{f_{(s_k,n)}[f_{p_1}^*(x_{r_1}^*)(\alpha_1)]: \alpha \in \alpha_1 \hat{\circ} (s_k,n)\}$$

Thus $f_p^*(x_{r_1}^*)(\alpha)$ is defined iff there exists $\alpha_1 \in \hat{\Gamma}$ such that $\alpha \in \alpha_1 \hat{\circ} (s_k,n)$ and $f_{p_1}^*(x_{r_1}^*)(\alpha_1)$ is defined. By inductive hypothesis, this is true iff there exists $\alpha_1 \in \hat{CM}(p_1)$ and $\alpha \in \alpha_1 \hat{\circ} (s_k,n)$,

and, by the definition of $\hat{o}$ and $\hat{CM}$, this last assertion is true iff $\alpha \in \hat{CM}(p)$. Hence, applying the inductive hypothesis again,

$f^*_{p_1}(x^*_{r_1})(\alpha_1) = f_{p_1}(0)$, for all α_1 appearing in the above meet, so that this meet equals $f_{(s_k,n)}[f_{p_1}(0)] = f_p(0)$.

$$\text{Q.E.D.}$$

Remark: As previously noted, and can be seen, e.g. from the proof of the last lemma, use of an encoding scheme creates chances for propagation through paths which are not interprocedurally valid. However, our lemma shows that even if an execution path is encoded by more than one element of $\hat{\Gamma}$, all of these "tags" are associated with the same information, namely - $f_q(0)$. Thus information is propagated correctly along each path, only more paths are now acceptable for that propagation. These observations will be made more precise in what follows.

Lemma 6.4: For each $n \in N^*$, $IVP(r_1,n) \subseteq IAP(r_1,n)$.

Proof: Let $q \in IVP(r_1,n)$ for some $n \in N^*$. We will show, by induction on the length of q, that $\sigma(CM(q)) \in \hat{CM}(q)$, so that, by Lemma 6.1, $q \in IAP(r_1,n)$.

Our assertion is obvious if q is the null execution path. Suppose it is true for all paths whose length is less than some $k \geq 0$, and let $n \in N^*$, $q \in IVP(r_1,n)$ whose length is k. Write $q = q_1 || (m,n)$. By inductive hypothesis, $\sigma(CM(q_1)) \in \hat{CM}(q_1)$. Now, three cases are possible:

(a) $(m,n) \in E^o$. In this case $\hat{CM}(q) = \hat{CM}(q_1)$ and $CM(q) = CM(q_1)$ so that $\sigma(CM(q)) \in \hat{CM}(q)$.

(b) (m,n) is a call edge. Then, by definition, $\hat{CM}(q)$ contains

$\sigma(CM(q_1)) * \sigma(m) = \sigma(CM(q))$

(c) (m,n) is a return edge. Let (c',r_p) denote the corresponding call edge. Since $q \in IVP(r_1,n)$, q can be decomposed as $q' || (c',r_p) || q'' || (m,n)$, where $q' \in IVP(r_1,c')$ and $q'' \in IVP_0(r_p,m)$. It is evident from the definitions of the quantities involved that that $CM(q) = CM(q')$ and that $CM(q_1) = CM(q') || (c')$. Hence $\sigma(CM(q_1)) = \sigma(CM(q)) * \sigma(c')$. It thus follows that $\sigma(CM(q))$ is a member of the set $\{\beta \in ECS(p) | \beta * \sigma(c') = \sigma(CM(q_1))\}$ which, by definition, is a subset of $\hat{CM}(q)$.

Q.E.D.

We can now state an analog of Theorem 4.6:

Theorem 6.5: (a) If (L,F) is a distributive data-flow framework then, for each $n \in N^*$

$$\hat{x}_n = \bigwedge \{f_p(0) : p \in IAP(r_1,n)\} \leq y_n$$

(b) If (L,F) is only monotone, then, for each $n \in N^*$

$$\hat{x}_n \leq \bigwedge \{f_p(0) : p \in IAP(r_1,n)\} \leq y_n$$

Proof: (a) Let $\alpha \in \hat{\Gamma}$. By Theorem 6.2 and Lemmas 6.1 and 6.3, we have

$$x_n^*(\alpha) = \bigwedge \{f_p^*(x_{r_1}^*)(\alpha) : p \in path_{G^*}(r_1,n)\}$$

$$= \bigwedge \{f_p(0) : p \in IAP(r_1,n), \alpha \in \hat{CM}(p)\}$$

Thus, by (6.3)

$$\hat{x}_n = \bigwedge_{\alpha \in \hat{\Gamma}} x_n^*(\alpha) = \bigwedge \{f_p(0) : p \in IAP(r_1,n)\}$$

By Lemma 6.4, this is

$$\leq \bigwedge \{f_p(0) : p \in IVP(r_1, n)\} = y_n$$

proving (a).

(b) Can be proved in a manner completely analogous to the proof of (a), using part (b) of Theorem 6.2.

Q.E.D.

Thus $\{\hat{x}_n\}_{n \in N*}$ is an under-estimation of the meet over all paths solution $\{y_n\}_{n \in N*}$. The degree of under-estimation depends on the deviation of $IAP(r_1, n)$ from $IVP(r_1, n)$, and this deviation is in turn determined by the choice of $\hat{\Gamma}$, * and σ. The most extreme under-estimation results if we let $IAP(r_1, n) = path_{G*}(r_1, n)$ for all $n \in N*$, i.e. define $\hat{\Gamma} = \{w\}$, $w*w = w$, and let σ map all calls to w. If we do this then the resulting problem is essentially equivalent to a purely intra-procedural analysis, in which procedure calls and returns are interpreted as mere branch instructions.

Another more interesting encoding scheme is as follows. Choose some integer $k > 1$, and let $\hat{\Gamma}$ be the ring of residue classes modulo k. Let $m > 1$ be another integer. For each $\alpha_1, \alpha_2 \in \hat{\Gamma}$, define $\alpha_1 * \alpha_2 = m \cdot \alpha_1 + \alpha_2 \pmod{k}$. Let σ be any map which maps call blocks to values between 0 and m-1 (preferably in a one-one way). In this scheme, call strings are mapped into a base m representation modulo k of some encoding of their call blocks. Note that if $k = \infty$, i.e. if we operate with integers rather than in modular arithmetic, then $\hat{\Gamma}$ and Γ are isomorphic, with * corresponding to concatenation. If $k = m^j$, for some $j \geq 1$, and σ is one-one and does not map any call block to 0, then the encoding scheme just proposed can roughly be described as follows: Keep only the last j calls within each call

string. As long as the length of a call string is less than j,
update it as in Section 4. However, if q is a call string of
length j, then, when appending to it a call edge, discard the first
component of q and add the new call block to its end. When appending a return edge, check if it matches the last call in q and, if
it does, delete this call from q and add to its start all possible
call blocks which call the procedure containing the first call in q.
This approximation may be termed a <u>call-string suffix approximation</u>.

At present we do not have available a comprehensive theory of
the proper choice of an encoding scheme. Appropriate choice of
such a scheme may depend on the program being analyzed, and
reflects the trade-off between tolerable complexity of the inter-
procedural analysis and some desired level of accuracy.

References

[AU]   Aho, A.V. and Ullman, J.D., "Principles of Compiler Design", Addison-Wesley 1977.

[AL1]   Allen, F.E., "Program Optimization", Annual Review of Automatic Programming 5(1969), 239-307.

[AL2]   Allen, F.E., "Interprocedural Data Flow Analysis", Proc. IFIP(1974) North-Holland, 398-402.

[AL3]   Allen, F.E. et al, "The Experimental Compiling System Project", IBM Research Report RC-6718, Yorktown Heights 1977.

[AC]   Allen, F.E. and Cocke, J., "A Program Data-Flow Analysis Procedure", CACM 19(1976) 137-147.

[BA]   Barth, J.M., "An Interprocedural Data Flow Analysis Algorithm", Proc. 4th ACM Symposium on Principles of Programming Languages (1977) 119-131.

[CO]   Cousot, P. and Cousot, R., "Static Determination of Dynamic Properties of Recursive Procedures", IFIP Conference on Formal Description of Programming Concepts, Saint Andrews(1977)

[DM]   DeBakker, J.W. and Meertens, L.G.L.T., "On the Completeness of the Inductive Assertion Method", Journal of Computer and Systems Science 11(1975) 323-357.

[GA]   Gallier, J.H., "Semantics and Correctness of Nondeterministic Flowchart Programs with Recursive Procedures", Fifth International Colloquium on Automata, Languages and Programming,

Udine, Italy(1978)

[GW]   Graham, S.L. and Wegman, M., "A Fast and Usually Linear Algorithm for Global Flow Analysis", JACM 23(1976) 172-202.

[GR]   Greibach, S.A., "Theory of Program Structure: Schemes, Semantics, Verification," Lecture Notes in Computer Science 36(1975), Springer Verlag.

[HA]   Harel, D., Pnueli, A. and Stavi, J., "Completeness Issues for Inductive Assertions and Hoare's Method", CS Tech. Rep., Tel Aviv University 1976.

[HE]   Hecht, M.S., "Flow Analysis of Computer Programs", Elsevier North-Holland, New York 1977.

[HU]   Hecht, M.S. and Ullman, J.D., "A Simple Algorithm for Global Data Flow Analysis Problems", SIAM J. Computing 4(1975) 519-532.

[KU1]   Kam, J.B. and Ullman, J.D., "Monotone Data Flow Analysis Frameworks", Tech. Rep. 169, Princeton University, N.J. 1975

[KU2]   Kam, J.B. and Ullman, J.D., "Global Data-Flow Analysis and Iterative Algorithms", JACM 23(1976) 158-171.

[KI]   Kildall, G.A., "A Unified Approach to Global Program Optimization", Proc. 1st ACM Symposium on Principles of Programming Languages (1973) 194-206

[LO]   Lomet, D.B., "Data Flow Analysis in the Presence of Procedure Calls", IBM Research Report RC-5728, Yorktown Heights 1975.

[MA]   Manna, Z., "Mathematical Theory of Computation", McGraw-Hill
       1974.

[RO]   Rosen, B.K., "Data Flow Analysis for Procedural Languages",
       IBM Research Report RC-5948, Yorktown Heights 1976.

[SH]   Sharir, M., "A Few Cautionary Remarks on the Convergence of
       Iterative Data-Flow Analysis Algorithms", SETL Newsletter 208,
       Courant Institute 1978.

[TA1] Tarjan, R.E., "Iterative Algorithms for Global Flow Analysis",
       Algorithms and Complexity, New Directions and Recent Results,
       Academic Press 1976.

[TA2] Tarjan, R.E., "Solving Path Problems on Directed Graphs",
       Tech. Rep. CS-75-512, Stanford University 1975.